FRENCH FOREIGN POLICY UNDER DE GAULLE

FRENCH FOREIGN POLICY UNDER DE GAULLE

ALFRED GROSSER

Université de Paris

Translated by Lois Ames Pattison

 LITTLE, BROWN AND COMPANY
Boston and Toronto

LIBRARY OF CONGRESS CATALOG CARD NO. 67–15419

FIRST PRINTING

*Published simultaneously in Canada
by Little, Brown & Company (Canada) Limited*

PRINTED IN THE UNITED STATES OF AMERICA

This book is a revision of *La Politique
extérieure de la Cinquième République.*
The chapter "And Now . . . " was written
especially for the English version.

FOREWORD

The study of politics in France — as in many countries in Europe —
has had trouble establishing its intellectual autonomy and finding
a place in the chilly sun of an antiquated academic structure. To a
large extent, the battle has been won, thanks to the brilliant works,
the diligence, and the devotion of a small group of men: the scholars and teachers of the Rue Saint Guillaume (the narrow street
where the undergraduate Institut d'Études Politiques of Paris, the
graduate Cycle d'Études Supérieures, and their research and publications center: the Fondation Nationale des Sciences Politiques have
their quarters).

These men were not trained as political scientists; they are historians, lawyers, economists, sociologists, civil servants with an interest in politics, all asking about the political process questions that
— strangely enough for a country so long and thoroughly mari-
nated in politics — very few scholars had asked before. Whatever
their formal training, these men have rescued the study of politics
from the routine of a purely historical approach and from the dis-
tortions of a purely legal viewpoint. In this respect, postwar Rue
Saint Guillaume is the collective heir of Tocqueville and of André
Siegfried, the collective colleague of Raymond Aron at the Sor-
bonne. The investigation of patterns of behavior, rather than
normative rules; of the social bases of interest groups in politics,
rather than merely parliamentary phenomena; of ideological ration-

alizations, opinion changes, and electoral trends rather than or in addition to electoral geography and political philosophy: such have been the major contributions of those men. More diffident of abstract schemes, closer to empirical data, and less concerned with developing systematic empirical theory than American political scientists, they have nevertheless also shown both their interest and their skill in this area, as the names Maurice Duverger and Jean Meynaud suggest. Above all, they have made an invaluable effort to deepen and broaden our knowledge of French politics in the largest sense: men like François Goguel, Řéné Rémond, Raoul Girardet, Georges Lavau, Jean Touchard have put "French experts" everywhere in their debt. Now, a new generation of political scientists, trained as political scientists, is emerging under the guidance of the "older" generation — the latter being composed of men in their forties and early fifties.

Among the pioneers of that older generation, no scholar has been more dynamic than Alfred Grosser, the youngest of the group. Born in Germany, he came to France as a child. France's capacity for total cultural assimilation is equaled only by that of the United States: many of France's social scientists came from Central and Eastern Europe, yet one would never have any clue if one did not know it as a fact. Trained as a "germaniste" — a specialist in German linguistics — Grosser soon developed a devouring interest for German history and politics, and became one of France's foremost scholars in that field, as well as one of the best teachers at the Institut d'Études Politiques. Soon, his concern for the quality of French political life, his moral and civic anguish as the citizen of a deeply disturbed polity, made him turn to the study of French politics. Today, Alfred Grosser is Director of Studies in the graduate program of the Rue Saint Guillaume, as well as professor at its Institut. He teaches also at the Bologna branch of Johns Hopkins University. He is a member of the office which, under the famous Franco-German treaty of 1963, is in charge of developing youth activities between the two countries (an abiding interest of his). For years, he has been the mainstay of a committee for exchanges with the new Germany. He has become a regular contributor to *Le Monde* and writes on foreign policy in the Catholic daily *La Croix*. He has taught at Stanford University during three quarters of 1965, and has been a frequent visitor at Harvard.

A prolific writer, his main characteristics are, first, a sophisticated, sinuous, and subtle intelligence of political events and motivations, which allows him both to go infallibly to the heart of an issue and to illuminate its ramifications, peculiarities, or paradoxes; second, a scrupulous and passionate sense of "fairness" which makes him not merely a reliable and compassionate scholar but also a stern if understanding judge of political behavior, of civic vagaries and partisan divagations. These qualities pervade all his writings, and especially his two principal books, neither of which has been published in English, due to the mysteries of translations and publishers: a masterful study of postwar Germany, *La Démocratie de Bonn* (1958), and a scholarly analysis of French foreign policy from 1944 to 1958, *La Quatrième République et la politique extérieure* (1961), a perfect example of what a scrutiny of the domestic roots of foreign policy making can be; a perfect demonstration of the influence domestic institutions and political style can exert on external relations.

The reader will find the same qualities in this book. Based on a lecture course at the Institut d'Études Politiques, published in 1965 in Paris by the Éditions du Seuil, it is a sequel to Grosser's earlier volume on French foreign policy. It differs from this previous study in that it does not contain a systematic analysis of the political forces: parties, institutions, pressure groups, press, etc. The reason is obvious: foreign policy under the Fourth Republic was the product of a complex bargaining process; foreign policy in the Fifth Republic is the expression of one man's vision, will, and statecraft. This does not mean, as many Americans believe, that the French nation merely tolerates this policy as a price to be paid in exchange for peace and prosperity. Grosser's book, balanced and objective, should help dispel this illusion. There is no doubt about the basic difference between the foreign policy-making process in the two regimes; yet this very contrast should make one pay more rather than less attention to the very broad areas of continuity. The Fifth

Republic has been neither as anti-European nor even as anti-American as Americans sometimes believe; the Fourth Republic had not been as satisfied and satisfying a NATO ally, as unconditionally in favor of European integration, as Americans sometimes remember. The hope for an end to the cold war in Europe that would allow for a reunification of the continent and make unnecessary what de Gaulle calls the "two hegemonies," the desire for a West European entity under French leadership, mixed feelings toward the United Nations, a drive for rank as well as nuclear power: there are powerfully persistent elements.

Alfred Grosser answers many of the questions which critics of de Gaulle always raise. He shows that behind the occasional inconsistencies, there is an obstinate vision: a new international system, still based on the nation-state as the basic actor, yet no longer bipolar, a system dominated neither by two superpowers in collision nor by two superpowers in collusion, but by a concert of very large and middle powers, in charge of preserving peace through a most classical mixture of mutual deterrence (now nuclear) and cooperation, a system acceptable to the lesser powers both because the game of balance among the great would safeguard the autonomy of the small, and because the great would learn to respect the independence of the small in the very interest of peace. Needless to say, the realization of such a vision would mean a return of France to higher rank. In serving this vision, de Gaulle has steadfastly pursued the same objectives (shaking up the hegemonies, preventing any irrevocable loss of French independence, assuring French security as much as possible through self-help, etc.). He has also pragmatically tried, one after the other or simultaneously, a dazzling variety of policies. What appears to the critic as a contradiction or discontinuity is merely the attempt by a skillful statesman to try as many approaches as he deems necessary in order to get nearer the very distant goals which his own power position does not allow him to reach directly, easily, or fast. If one approach fails, another will be attempted; often, conflicting alternatives are pursued at the same ·time, both because they point in the same direction in the long run, and because if one of them should lead into a dead end one would then still have a number of cards to play.

Grosser offers a more elusive answer to two other questions often raised by critics: Is de Gaulle's policy realistic or anachronistic? Is it good or bad? Those who deem it anachronistic object mainly to de Gaulle's faith in the nation-state, which they consider to be obsolete and nefarious. They reject his conception of world politics as a game in which each actor ought to behave in such a way as never to disappear from it. Grosser obviously sympathizes with the critics, yet he knows and shows that all too often the only choice a statesman faces is between the assertion of his will and his subordination to someone else's, not between the survival of his nation and its transcendence in a larger and higher entity. Moreover, de Gaulle's recognition of the role and needs of the new nations, his understanding of the effect of nuclear weapons on the bipolar contest and on alliances, show a capacity to exploit and accelerate new trends in world affairs which can hardly be called anachronistic and which contrast with some of his attitudes of the middle and late 1940's. The earlier de Gaulle, dissatisfied with the order that emerged from World War II, thought too much of restoring the old pre-Hitler order; the de Gaulle of today still wants to shake the postwar order, but by exploiting the very germs of change it contains.

A moral judgment of de Gaulle's policy is even more difficult than a judgment of its realism. For a first question would be: good for whom? Those who point out that his concern for the good of France apparently rules out the good of mankind or of broader communities still have to demonstrate that the latter would have been better served by another policy, and can in practice be separated from the good of specific nations. Also, one would have to separate a judgment of the ends — questionable but hardly evil — and a judgment of the means — for which no one has anything kind to say and which seem, at times, so brutal as to be incapable of reaching the desired ends. Yet what if the long run ends were not reachable in any other way, if gentler means turned out to be too soft for the kinds of changes in world affairs de Gaulle tries to obtain? Moreover, ethical judgments in politics have to look at consequences, not merely at ends and means, and, here again, it is hard to judge: for what is it that weighs more heavily, the contribution to a thaw between East and West in Europe, to decolonization and cooperation between France and the new nations, or the decline in community spirit between France and her allies, the risk of a nationalist contagion?

The moral censors of de Gaulle, the deplorers of his anachronism, converge to attack what they consider his major error: his belief that in the present world a nation of France's size and resources can still play an important role. This they denounce as *hubris,* and they see in it a grave danger precisely because other national leaders, less prudent perhaps, might make the same mistake with worse results. We cannot say whether these critics are right or wrong until the returns are in, until the consequences have become clear. In other words, the decisive question is that of de Gaulle's ultimate success or failure — for surely a chaotic world of nationalist epidemics would not fulfill his vision, any more than would a perpetuation of the "hegemonies" and of Europe's division or a failure to get other Europeans (West and East) to move in his preferred direction.

As of now, the question cannot be answered. All too often, it has seemed as if de Gaulle had failed — yet a short-term setback or delay only prefaced or prepared a long-term success. Grosser is critical of the political yield of the *force de frappe,* of de Gaulle's fiasco in European political integration and in Franco-German relations. My own judgment would be more hesitant, for a variety of reasons. First, a short-term failure has a good chance of being erased if long-term trends and (or) the mistakes of others later play into one's hands. This is obviously what de Gaulle has counted on. The evolution of America's policy in Europe may well prove him right: the weight of the US in German policy, which he has reenforced at first through his brutality, risks being reduced by America's own moves — precisely those he had always expected. Second, in an international system in which the most bluntly effective agent of change, the use of force, has been blunted, success or failure become much more difficult to assess. In a way, nobody fails or succeeds entirely, and there is always room for appeal and maneuver. Precisely what de Gaulle has understood best is the leeway which the new conditions of the use of force give to middle powers, the opportunities which exist when the tangible material ingredients of power of which France has only a small supply, while indispensable, cannot, however, be translated directly or immediately into influence, when influence depends also on intangibles that are far more evenly distributed than those material elements. Third, since success or failure are much more uncertain, and because influence depends on skill as much as on insight, the figure one cuts in playing the game, one's reputation as a player, one's personal prestige and sense of drama, the spectacle one gives, and the symbols one manipulates become conditions of any success and also carry their own rewards. When the payoff is unsure, the show is the business. It is not proven that those who have been self-effacing and who have, for instance, tried to influence Washington by loyalty, docility, or soft advice, have been any more successful than the dramatic artist of the Élysée Palace.

To be sure, if the only result of his artistry should be an American disengagement from Europe and the kind of political vacuum in Europe that would consolidate the Soviet hold in the East and encourage West Germany to stage her own nationalist revival, de Gaulle's policy will have to be judged severely. But the worst is not sure. In 1965, he tried to slow down a supranational integration of Western Europe which he deemed deceptive; in this respect (here I somewhat disagree with Grosser) he succeeded. But the compromise that ended the crisis not only left the communities standing, it also strengthened common policies and thus tightened bonds between France and Germany. In other words, de Gaulle's policy, for all its unpleasantness, has perhaps "insulted" but certainly not destroyed the future. The returns are not in.

One thing is clear — and here again we return to the basic, obvious fact: the personal style of the General gives its special shape to a policy which, in its aspirations and connotations, corresponds to French desires. It is a policy that dares to take risks, to gamble for high stakes, to court failure rather than resigning itself to mediocrity and timidity. The various alternatives pursued, to the bewilderment of many, do not express a refusal to choose, a cautious desire to play it safe — they express a statecraft that, precisely because the goal is high and remote, needs to try every approach toward a clearly designed goal. As Grosser points out, such a policy has met with the approval of most of the French. A kind of trickling down of Gaullism has marked the views even of the opposition parties, especially on the left. No foreign critic of de Gaulle should forget the contribution his policy has made to forging a domestic consensus, after years of discord in which foreign policy divergences played a large part. Yet even if what is good for France should be good for the world, as de Gaulle obviously believes; even if the trends in world affairs should move in a direction that spells success rather than failure for his policies, the problem of ultimate success will remain unsettled for a long time to come. For, just because the gamble is so daring and the aim so far away, the prospect of reaching the promised land so small in de Gaulle's lifetime, ultimate success will depend not only on external events during his remaining years and the years of his successor, but also on his successors' capacity to pursue his policies with the same skill and vigor. The domestic Achilles' heel is even tenderer than the external one; the greatest unknown remains the French one.

Should the critics of de Gaulle wish for domestic turmoil and mediocrity so as to be vindicated in their predictions of chaos and fiasco? Shouldn't they rather hope that after de Gaulle, French leaders will save the essence of his work — the double effort to preserve the nation from wasteful and untenable commitments, and to provide her nevertheless with new cards to play and new ambitions of which she could be proud? Those who deem those cards false and those ambitions excessive, who believe that the only true alternative to the old obsolete commitments would be a supranational ambition, have never proven that the latter could, at the present time, be sure not to turn into a delusion, a trap, or a premature dream. Nor have they established that de Gaulle's policies have definitely forsaken rather than raised the chances of a future integrative evolution that would be based on a genuine European *prise de conscience,* and not be an exercise in confusion or an escape from politics. Until the returns are in, judgment must be suspended. In the meantime, Grosser's admirable study will help us evaluate what has been achieved so far.

STANLEY HOFFMANN

TABLE OF CONTENTS

xiii

FRENCH FOREIGN POLICY
UNDER DE GAULLE

I

THE RECORD OF
THE FOURTH REPUBLIC

The Goals of 1944 and the Goals of 1947

How may a political record be evaluated? How does one judge a policy? One sort of evaluation is always possible: has the policy attained the goals for which it was intended? Was there a homogeneity, a correlation, between the desired ends and the means utilized to achieve them? It is on the basis of this criterion that I should like to evaluate the record of the Fourth Republic. But first of all, I must explain why I attach less importance today than I did several years ago, when I was writing *La Quatrième République et sa politique extérieure,*[1] to another criterion — the value of foreign policy[2] as compared to domestic politics.

At that point, indeed, I had noticed a great difference between

[1] Paris, A. Colin, 1961.
[2] In French, there is a difference between "politique étrangère" and "politique extérieure." As long as Algeria was French, as long as France dominated Vietnam or Black Africa, or, more briefly, as long as decolonization was on the way, this decolonization was "politique extérieure" but definitely not "politique étrangère."

General de Gaulle from 1944–46, on the one hand, and the Fourth
Republic, on the other — in the fact that foreign policy was pre-
dominant in General de Gaulle's political thinking as a whole, while
most of the Fourth Republic leaders were preoccupied with domestic concerns. Obviously, this sheds a different light on foreign policy.
However, upon more sober reflection, can one really come to any
other conclusion than that the political life of the Fourth Republic
was primarily and basically dominated by foreign policy?

Not even one month before the institutions of the Fourth Republic began to work in January, 1947, war had started in Indo-
China. A couple of weeks later, the East-West split provoked the
communists' expulsion from the cabinet on May 5, and, after the
Cominform was created early in October, there followed the violent fight put up by the communist party and the communist-dom-
inated unions against the other parties, "Slaves of the American
imperialists." And there was to be hardly any respite. From 1951 on,
it might be said that nearly all the Governments fell — even if
appearances were often to the contrary — because of underlying
permanent crises in foreign policy: Europe, German rearmament,
Indochina, and from 1954 on, Algeria. It was finally over a Tuni-
sian-Algerian issue that the Republic itself broke down in May,
1958. Consequently, I do not feel that it is altogether correct to
maintain that foreign policy was not the Fourth Republic's principal preoccupation. The great distinction that one might make is
that the Fourth Republic was preoccupied by foreign policy out of
necessity, while General de Gaulle's preoccupation was one of taste.
But in truth, the fundamental preoccupation with foreign policy was
permanent.

I should like to point out that there was at the outset a conflict
between what one might call two groups of objectives:

The goals of 1944: "status" and security vis-à-vis Germany.
The goals of 1947: the necessity of restoring prosperity through
foreign aid, and security vis-à-vis the Soviet Union.

The combination of these two goals from 1947 on takes shape
in "Europe."

Before examining these two groups of goals, it must be noted that one contradictory element is common to both groups: *the problem of the Empire,* which had become the French Union. The contradiction between the myth of Brazzaville and the reality of the texts signed in Brazzaville, the contradiction between the liberal spirit of the Preamble to the Constitution of 1946 and the absence of liberalism in Title VIII of the same Constitution, weighed heavily in the years 1945–58.[3] But if we return to the two groups of goals pair by pair, we shall see that even within them there are contradictions. Security toward Germany, as defined in 1944 and continued under the Fourth Republic, was hardly reconcilable with the preoccupation of security vis-à-vis the Soviet Union. It was many years before some attempt was made to eliminate the friction between these two goals, and during those years foreign policy sought to satisfy ʻsimultaneously the preoccupation with security toward Germany and security toward the East.

A second conflict in goals: independence, on the one hand; and prosperity, on the other. Without Marshall Plan aid, there could be no rapid build-up of the French economy. At the time, there was much discussion over whether there was not really some means other than Marshall Plan aid. There was even some question of whether Marshall Plan aid was, in the final analysis, beneficial to the French economy. Today, no one denies any longer that Marshall Plan aid very plainly helped the French economy to get off the ground again, and above all made possible the success of the First French Plan initiated by Jean Monnet in 1946 — particularly since Marshall Plan aid was invested in heavy industry.

Similarly, no one questions that security was achieved by Atlantic policy. But acceptance of both the requested aid and military protection in effect required renouncing the independent status included in the goals of 1944. Discussion becomes difficult here because one must inquire whether security is one of the essential and

---

[3] At a conference convened at General de Gaulle's initiative, in Brazzaville (French Congo) in January, 1944, to consider the future of the French Empire, the final decisions had not been very liberal (see Chapter IV). But ever since that time, the Brazzaville conference has been considered as the beginning of decolonization.

permanent elements of independence. We shall encounter this problem continually under the Fifth Republic: If there is no security against the threat from the East, independence is lost toward the East. But does not acceptance of American protection entail surrendering part of one's independence toward the West in order to remain independent from the East? In other words, what concessions in independence must be made toward the United States in order to ensure the priority of independence toward the East?

From 1947 on, an underlying theme of French foreign policy was a sort of permanent dream: "If only there were no longer anything like the threat from the East!" For, in that case, relations with the United States would be profoundly transformed, and the old and more satisfying independence would be restored. We encounter this dream, voiced at times, but more often implicit, as the major political preoccupation of the Fifth Republic.

But independence is also opposed to prosperity, and to "Europe." As early as 1947, in the first proclamation of the European countries requesting Marshall Plan aid — at the meeting that gave birth to the OEEC — the preliminary affirmation stated that each of the countries was dependent on a broader European organization, on the setting up of a European community. Is the promotion of a community favoring national prosperity the same as renouncing independence? We must then raise a parenthetical question: Prosperity, for what? The reply of the Fourth Republic was incontestably: So that the people might be prosperous. The reply of the Fifth Republic would be more like this: So that prosperity should forge the means of foreign policy. Hence, the very notion of prosperity would not be altogether the same under the two regimes. But in any case, even in the perspective of the Fifth Republic, it was necessary back in 1948–50 to answer the question: What concessions of French autonomy must be made to other European countries in order to promote national prosperity? Similarly, can a weakened country's possibilities for action be increased by its membership in a wider community called "Europe"? At the time, there was conflict over whether it was necessary to renounce some sovereignty in order to acquire, through an intermediary person or a superior unit, wider possibilities of action than if one retained national sovereignty intact. This tension runs through the whole Fourth Republic, and we shall see it emerge in an identical fashion under the Fifth Republic.

The Major Choices

With these tensions between the goals of 1944 and those of 1947 in mind, we might inquire what major choices in foreign policy were made during the Fourth Republic.

A preliminary remark: Were these voluntary choices, or choices passively *submitted to?* This is very difficult to assess. A number of choices were made under the Fourth Republic that were definitely acts of will: the Schuman Plan, leading to the creation of a European community for coal and steel; Mendès-France's trip to Tunisia in July, 1954, reversing the harsh policy into one of confidence and liberalism; the *Loi-cadre* of Gaston Defferre in 1956, giving the framework for a peaceful evolution toward autonomy; and the Common Market, which started with the *relance* of 1955 under Edgar Faure. Others were incontestably surrenders after long rearguard struggle — German rearmament, for instance. This does not mean that it is easy to draw a line between what was voluntary and what was submitted to. Even in the most positive decisions, there is a note of resignation, of submission to a reality that does not appear altogether pleasant. This is true of the Schuman Plan, where, alongside the creative aspect, there is this one: "How can we continue to control the German coal and steel industry now that Germany is in the process of becoming independent again?"

Likewise, in Mendès-France's trip to Tunis, there is this aspect: "Let's attempt to present as an act of will what appears to be an irreversible evolution." The same holds for the *Loi-cadre*. Scarcely any issue, aside from the Common Market, creates the impression of an unambiguous initiative, a creative will that is not necessarily dictated by the reality of the moment. Contrariwise, were a certain number of apparent renunciations really renunciations, or were they rather a bringing into harmony of political wisdom and reality?

It appears to me that four major choices were made by the Fourth Republic:

Atlantic Solidarity ("Atlantisme"). The decision to take a position in the struggle between the two camps was first made at the Moscow Conference in April, 1947, gradually confirmed subsequently, and definitively established with the Atlantic Alliance on April 4, 1949. In retrospect, this choice seems clear, even though undoubtedly it did not correspond to the deepest aspirations of the population, because one encounters continually in the statements of leaders, in opinion polls, and in the press a sort of permanent longing: "If only we could get rid of both of the Big Two at once!" This resigned acceptance of the division of the world, and the recognition of the fact that one belongs to one camp in opposition to another, hardly seems to arouse political passion. The decision is motivated more by a recognition of the ineluctable than by a priority in foreign policy accorded to the division of the world into two camps.

The Transformation of Franco-German Relations. Here, the reversal is so plain that we go virtually from "no enemy, but Germany," in 1944, to "no friend, but Germany," in 1958. When the Fourth Republic fell in 1958, relations between France and the Federal Republic had taken on a particularly cordial tone. What was missing after the first Franco-German "wave" — that of the small minority of pioneers from 1945–49 — and the second "wave," toward 1950 with Robert Schuman, was the *ralliement* of the French nationalist tradition. This was the *"nouvelle vague"* of the Fifth Republic: General de Gaulle won over the Franco-German rapprochement in 1958 an unconverted sector — that of the Jacobin tradition of the Left, and the tradition of Barrès and Bainville on the Right.[4]

"Europe." In theory, the choice was made in 1950 with the Schuman Plan, but until the very end, there was a good amount of confusion over the decision's implications.

Decolonization. It is not altogether certain that this was a global

---

[4] See Chapter V for further explanations of these events.

decision rather than a case of gradual concessions to localized territories.

Reluctant Choices

Having pointed out the four major choices, we must now consider to what extent they represented reluctant decisions. So far as the decision in favor of Atlanticism was concerned, at least two elements made this a reluctant choice. From one end to the other, from 1947–49 until 1958, the element of anti-Americanism, springing from a feeling of dependence, seems undeniable to me. This anti-Americanism grew stronger with the impression of greater dependence on the United States. The first period was that of the Marshall Plan and the American aid in Indo-China, and the second that of the loss of Indo-China and the problems in North Africa — accompanied by the feeling of being a country in decline, while the United States was a rising country. The second element of malaise involved in the Atlantic choice was based on the impression that the United States would not guarantee French security when certain actions, rightly or wrongly deemed essential to French security, ran counter to American policy — such as the Suez expedition in 1956 and even the Algerian war. The virtual fusion of the two defense systems — French national defense and global Western defense — appeared deplorable, and one notes clearly the growth of regret at having subordinated the national defense system to a global Atlantic defense system defined by the United States. This was to be one of the causes of the "coup" of May 13, 1958 that brought de Gaulle back to power.

At the same time, even within the Atlantic security system, after having begged the United States not to make inconsidered use of the nuclear threat from 1950–52, beginning in 1954, the contrary came to be true and the French Government endeavored to persuade the United States not to renounce its reliance on the nuclear threat — that is, from the time when the Soviet Union was capable of striking American territory. Out of this grew the question of whether American protection, or "strategic Atlanticism," could guarantee European security any longer, assuming that no American President would be willing to risk suicide for the defense of Europe.

Consequently, under the last Governments of the Fourth Republic, there emerged the conviction, first formulated by Edgar Faure, that nothing must be said or done that would compromise France's freedom to develop atomic weapons. Then, step by step, the decision was made to build a French atomic force.

The decision on German policy prompts very few regrets. Hesitations do, nonetheless, remain, and the temptation to consider Germany as an object of international politics, whose manipulation might open the door to a desirable détente with the Soviet Union, has certainly not disappeared. An unexpressed malaise persists in Franco-German relations: how sincere are the French in supporting Berlin policy or reunification? On the French side: How much faith should be placed in German assurances of the definitive integration of Germany with the West? Distrust is far from being entirely dead on either side.

As for Europe, the choice was made, in principle; but the economic and financial consequences of the choice were not implemented. Thus, when the Fourth Republic died, the foreign financial status of France was such that no one believed the Common Market could begin operating without France's immediately requesting application of the safeguard clause, because the grave deficits in net commercial balance and in net balance of payments would have prevented her from implementing the stipulations of the treaty. On the other hand, there remained a strong feeling against supranationalism. The renunciation of parcels of sovereignty had been justified by arguments based on national interest. But from 1953 on, European political integration was blocked by French policy, as formulated at the time by Georges Bidault. The possibility of arriving at a supranational authority was set aside as early as 1953, on French initiative. The *relance européenne* (new start of a European policy) of 1955 that culminated in the Treaty of Rome of 1957, creating the Common Market, was conceived as a detour — and, as such, long and difficult — in order to arrive finally at supranational political unification. The route was conceived as so long that its drafters did not dare to introduce into the text of the Economic Community the same dose of supranationality that had been inserted into the text of 1951 establishing the European Coal and Steel Community.

Finally, concerning the choice of decolonization, the record in 1958 seems to demonstrate that there was indeed an implicit decision, but not a wholly accepted one. The settlement of July, 1954 in Indo-China was followed by a considerable contraction of French positions in Southeast Asia. In North Africa, there was a reversal in relations with Tunisia and Morocco, and it is in the relations with these countries that the policy of presence without domination is best seen. In Black Africa, there was widespread agreement that the *Loi-cadre* was but a transitory measure, but there was little risk of a psychological obstacle here: the policy put into operation could, indeed, aim at decolonization. One even has the impression here that there was no major obstacle to a total reversal in policy, including a complete withdrawal, so great was the indifference of domestic opinion toward problems of Black Africa. This was hardly the beginning of a policy like that in Tunisia and Morocco, namely, the replacement of a policy of domination by one of presence. It seemed that the choice to be confronted in Black Africa in 1958 lay between domination and absence.

But the Fourth Republic died because there was a complete block over the last and most important problem: Algeria. Algeria was *not* treated as the final problem of overseas domination, to be considered under the rubric "decolonization." Not only did the Fourth Republic refuse to consider this possibility, but it denied that the choice even existed. Algeria was not a part of the territories to which the idea of decolonization applied. The men who were swept out of office following the coup of May 13 always declared, at least publicly, that they were in fundamental agreement with the men who removed them from office, and that the latter were in the wrong not to take their public pronouncements seriously. In retrospect, it has appeared to the great majority of French people that Algeria was indeed a problem of decolonization. Why was this not recognized earlier?

The Refusal of Adaptation:
The Debate over "Realism"

After considering the goals, the choices, the reluctant decisions, we now come to what was called the refusal to adapt to the modern world, which is considered by the best observers writing on France to have been the decisive factor in French foreign policy, and in French policy generally in the postwar period. Whether one reads Raymond Aron or Jean-Baptiste Duroselle, one major theme emerges: the refusal to adapt to the modern world. In this observation, of course, there are very strong elements of reality. The idea that France was dependent on certain vested interests, that France would no longer be France if it gave up a given position or traditional possession, was widely accepted throughout the whole Fourth Republic. It led to great outbursts of passion and a refusal even to consider that there were priorities, such as the East-West priority. For instance, in his *Lettre aux Américains*[5] written on the occasion of his election to the Académie Française, Thierry Maulnier concludes: "In North Africa, France is defending her last chance. Do not force her to choose between her African vocation and American friendship." This last sentence could only mean: "African vocation equals domination in Africa." It is thus true that there did exist a nationalism of resentment, and that there was a refusal of adaptation. And yet, I do not wholly agree with the thesis of Raymond Aron or Jean-Baptiste Duroselle, in that, it seems to me, they do not adequately define what they mean by adaptation to reality. In reading them, one gets the impression that there is only one reality and that what is at stake is deciding whether one will adapt to it or not. But it turns out that reality is, in part, what it is believed to be; *reality is, in part, what one makes it.* If we recognize it as different, we create a different reality. To define reality as renunciation is to begin that renunciation.

This appears to me to be the major difficulty of assessment in-

---

[5] The major points of this text are quoted in my book, *La Quatrième République*, p. 391, from *Figaro*, January 9, 1957.

volved in reproaching the Fourth Republic for refusing to adapt to the world, and the Fifth Republic for lack of realism. Where are the dividing lines? What is the criterion that distinguishes an unpardonable lack of realism that consists in pursuing a policy deemed to be bad because it is contrary to the facts of the real world, from an equally unpardonable policy of abdication which accepts submission to reality because it refuses to transform it? In other words, when is the affirmation of will an imprudent bet? When is the refusal to impose one's will an abdication? There is no sure criterion, no decisive dividing line, whether it concerns independence toward the United States or the creation of a Europe transcending nations. It is indeed for this reason that pronouncements of judgment on political decisions always contain an element of debate, of uncertainty, of opinion. At a given moment, one person might maintain that it was necessary to submit to reality; another might reply: "Perhaps it was because our will was not strong enough that we did not succeed in transforming reality and in shaping it to the goal that we sought to attain." In discussions of the Fifth Republic's foreign policy, this is one of the most decisive aspects, whether the question at issue concerns a well-publicized affirmation of will, or a less spectacular, but nonetheless certain renunciation.

The "Moral" Record

Before coming to the Fifth Republic, we must inquire into one last question about the Fourth Republic: What was its "moral" record? I mean by this: In what state did the Fourth Republic leave the French people? What opinion of itself did it give rise to in other countries? To begin with, domestically, 1958 marked, so to speak, the high point in domestic conflict over legitimacy, due to the interpenetration of two world conflicts and French domestic politics: decolonization vs. refusal to decolonize and the communist-anticommunist conflict. I believe that this theme is of supreme importance, though I shall not return to it: France was torn by both problems. To what extent were these conflicts really felt by the French people? My reply is that I do not know. Herein lies an almost insurmountable difficulty. How can the depth of the crises that seem decisive be measured when one takes account of political and ideological agitation? Was the battle over the EDC a deep-seated debate? "Certainly," I would have answered in 1954; "I don't believe so," I would have replied ten years later. Did the Algerian war really shake the national community? "Uncontestably," I would still have replied in autumn, 1962. But the return to calm within France has been so radical that one might indeed question whether the political scene had not been unduly dominated by unrepresentative minorities, when compared to the national community. We shall return to this question.

Insofar as French prestige abroad and the position of France in the world were concerned, the situation at the end of the Fourth Republic was complex. There was an almost universal astonishment at the stability within instability, at the permanence of European policy, at the Franco-German success. And there was widespread contempt for the financial disorder in particular, for, ten years after the Marshall Plan, France's financial mendicity had not in the least ended; quite the contrary. And finally, there was the refusal to yield to the reality of decolonization. When the Government — whatever Government — referred to the cultural and moral prestige of France, fatherland of freedom, etc., the phrase was not false; but what was striking in the situation was that, abroad, those who were called to speak in the name of the Eternal France of the Rights of Man were precisely those in opposition to French policy, precisely those who were accused of compromising national unity. The divorce between the power and the intellectual prestige of France, viewed from abroad, was considerable at the time. One might, nonetheless, ponder whether the situation had been different at any other time in history. We might raise this question again apropos the Fifth Republic.

II

THE CONCEPTIONS OF
GENERAL DE GAULLE

Why does this subject merit consideration? It is not merely because
the fundamental decisions of the Fourth Republic have allegedly
been modified under the Fifth. We shall have occasion later to consider whether or not the major choices that have been discussed
have in fact been modified under the Fifth Republic. The thesis
that I shall expound throughout this book is that none of the fundamental decisions of the Fourth Republic — although they were
often counter to General de Gaulle's position at the time — has
been really called into question under the Fifth Republic. But, there
has been a change in tone, a change in style, a change in the ideological inspiration of foreign policy. And finally, there has been a
change in the mechanisms of decision making. There is no doubt
that it is General de Gaulle himself who makes the decisions on
foreign policy issues.

Theoretically, his decisions are based on Article 52 of the Constitution: "the President of the Republic negotiates and ratifies treaties" — which is the text of 1875 — "he is informed of any nego-

tiation tending to the conclusion of an international accord not submitted to ratification" — this is a legacy of the Constitution of 1946.
Since he makes the major decisions concerning foreign policy, one
might conclude that the President of the Republic overshadows
the Prime Minister in this domain. Is this also true of the Minister
of Foreign Affairs?

In a number of books and commentaries — notably in the book
by Nora Beloff, *The General Says No* — Couve de Murville's role
is minimized to the point of labeling him "His Master's Voice." I
believe that the description in *Time* magazine, dedicated largely to
Monsieur Couve de Murville, is much closer to the truth. "In fact,"
writes *Time,* "Couve plays a much larger role than would appear at
first sight."[1] During the negotiations in Brussels in December, 1964,
notably, the French Minister of Foreign Affairs enjoyed much wider
power of acceptance or rejection than his foreign colleagues. The
President of the Republic establishes the major directions within
which the Minister of Foreign Affairs enjoys an appreciable latitude
of action.

Moreover, it is a fact that General de Gaulle's interest in a given
problem is intermittent — this is one of his techniques of governing. At times, he takes up a question; at other times, he takes no part
at all. In any case, General de Gaulle certainly exhibits a distrust of
diplomatic personnel, which he expressed in the second volume of
his *Mémoires* (which, by the way, I shall have occasion to quote
countless times) apropos the year 1945. But the expression seems to
me as valid for the period of the Fifth Republic as well: "First of
all, the personnel of our diplomatic corps concurred only remotely
with the attitude I had adopted. For many of the men in charge of
our foreign relations, concord with England was a kind of principle.
But between the impulse I was trying to transmit and the behavior
of those who actually wrote the notes, maintained the contacts and
established the communications, the discrepancy was too apparent
to escape our associates, thereby weakening the effect of my own

[1] February 7, 1964.

determination."[2] (Whence the necessity of keeping in line and maintaining close surveillance over French negotiators.)

The style, the inspiration, the monopoly over decisions, all contribute to the importance of studying the political thought and attitudes of General de Gaulle.

The Nation and National Ambition

We shall examine successively the idea of the nation and that of national ambition. Then we shall inquire whether the word *Realpolitik* is the one which best corresponds to the diplomatic method employed. Finally, we shall consider the man himself and his style of action and government.

If by "nationalist" one means a man for whom the nation represents the supreme political value, then General de Gaulle is a nationalist. This is not to imply any notion of aggressiveness, it is simply to emphasize the privileged position of the nation among his political concepts. This idea explains the primacy of foreign policy and the notion of national unity as the essential ideal of all domestic policy.

The State and the Primacy of Power. What is the state? "I regarded the state," wrote General de Gaulle, "not as it was yesterday and as the parties wished it to become once more, a juxtaposition of private interests which could never produce anything but weak compromise, but instead an instrument of decision, action and ambition, expressing and serving the national interest alone. In order to make decisions and determine measures, it must have a qualified arbitrator at its head."[3] In other words, the goal of the state is external ambition, and this is what justifies very broadly the presence at the helm of a person in possession of the power of the state, and capable of acting toward the world outside.

This is why the various ministerial departments are conceived as

---

[2] *The Complete War Memoirs of Charles de Gaulle*, translated by Jonathan Griffin and Richard Howard. New York: Simon and Schuster, 1964, pp. 890–891.

[3] *Ibid.*, p. 780.

a function of foreign policy. In refusing to allot one of the three major ministries to the communists in 1945 (the same ones that he refused to Jacques Soustelle in 1958), General de Gaulle explained himself as follows: "I did not feel it would be justifiable to entrust them with any of the three key foreign policy posts — Foreign Affairs, which expresses the policy, the War Office, which upholds it, or the Police, which protects it."[4] The Ministry of the Interior is seen less as an organ of administration than as an organ of public order making it possible to conduct foreign policy. Accordingly, almost all, if not all internal undertakings have a purpose in foreign policy. General de Gaulle recalls in his *Mémoires,* with a satisfaction that seems justified to me, the social works undertaken by the Provisional Government from 1944–46: legislation on tenant farming, social security, etc. But what led him to make this kind of decision? "Once again I remarked that if the goal was perhaps the same for them as for myself, the motives guiding them were not identical with my own. Though they adjusted their attitudes to accord with the prejudices of their respective tendencies, such considerations did not affect me. On the other hand, I perceived that they were scarcely aware of the motive inspiring me, which was the power of France."[5] The ultimate purpose of social security and legislation on tenant farming is the power of France.

The same inspiration underlies nearly all the texts of the Fifth Republic. Two examples will suffice. First, the New Year's message for 1963: "Our prosperity has reached a level that we have never known before, and we have realized unprecedented social progress. In proportion as expansion and reason lead us to power, France regains its status, its allure, its means." And again, in the message to the National Assembly on December 11, 1962: "To pursue the development of our country in such a manner as to enhance at the same time the condition of the individual, national prosperity, and the power of France."

[4] General de Gaulle, *War Memoirs, Salvation (1944–46), Documents,* translated by Joyce Murchie and Hamish Erskine. New York: Simon and Schuster, 1960, p. 363.
[5] *The Complete War Memoirs, op. cit.,* p. 779.

The French People and "France." The economy is a means. The prosperity of the French people is a means, especially in that they are not the objective of policy. The objective of policy is "France," which is very distinct from the sum of the French people, who are all engaged in its service. This explains a political attitude which scorns the various divisions between Frenchmen, or at least, which considers them inconsequential. In terminating his message to the Constituent Assembly on March 2, 1945, General de Gaulle exclaimed: "A single party or a new one? Certainly not! Not more so tomorrow than yesterday! They are good Frenchmen, of all opinions, origins and inclinations, who wherever they are, set the example of enthusiasm and act in such a manner that, in each of the political, social or professional sectors, they make their interests and passions subservient to the superior interests of France.[6]

This means, in other words, that all ideological and political divisions among Frenchmen are subordinate, of little moment, in relation to the national interest, which in turn is oriented toward foreign policy. It also implies that this national interest exists — in other words, that at any given moment, one can always define the interest of the national community in a plain, clear, and evident fashion. Finally, it also means that there can be no debate among citizens on what the national interest *is* at a given moment. The result or the consequence of this conception, as I have attempted to point out elsewhere, is to deprive politics of its highest substance — to permit citizens to choose among different conceptions of the national interest. It also leads politically to what I shall overstate in speaking of the "double nature" of each Frenchman. Each Frenchman has two souls. The one leads him to membership in social, economic, and political groups; through it, he belongs to a family, a religion, a profession, to everything that divides the French people. By virtue of the other soul he is a member of a united community and is represented by the President of the Republic, who defines what the national interest is by expressing what the French people, unconsciously, should conceive as being that interest.

[6] *War Memoirs. Salvation (1944–46), Documents, op. cit.,* pp. 185–186.

A Vision of International Affairs. Out of this notion of national interest, of the nation, and of the nation having ambitions in the outside world, there emerges a whole conception of international affairs. What is important and enduring in international affairs are nation-states, and not regimes and ideologies. Nation-states are not whatever is legally defined as such. It is clear that for General de Gaulle the African countries have not yet arrived at the nation-state stage. Some antiquity is required. Certain countries, like China, are "older than history" and are more specially nation-states. A certain age is required in order for a country to constitute a bona fide nation-state. In his press conference of January 31, 1964, General de Gaulle spoke of "the regime that *presently* dominates China." The regime is what is transitory. This in turn accounts for de Gaulle's conception of international relations based primarily on bilateral relationships. In December, 1944, when General de Gaulle was in Moscow negotiating the Franco-Soviet treaty with Stalin, he received a telegram from Churchill asking, "May I be a third party?", which would have made a tripartite pact. General de Gaulle became indignant and said to Stalin, according to the minutes of the meeting, "Between France and the Soviet Union, there is no object of direct contestation. With Great Britain, we always have had and always will have differences." Slightly less than twenty years later, in a newspaper interview — seemingly prompted by the Élysée — Edgar Faure declared: "The fact that the tensions which could exist between France and China no longer exist today . . ." etc.[7] This is the very same formula as with Stalin in 1944.

The factor of prime importance in the relations between nation-states is the bilateralism of their national interest. And a nation-state is only truly worthy of being one if it has an ambition. When General de Gaulle visited Germany in 1945, he wrote in a compassionate tone: "For many years, the ambitions of the German nation and the aims of its policy would necessarily be reduced to the level of survival and reconstruction."[8] These are meager enough for an important nation-state! We shall see subsequently to what extent

[7] *Figaro*, January 9, 1964.
[8] *The Complete War Memoirs, op. cit.*, p. 903.

this notion of national ambition is indispensable in explaining both the divergences within the Atlantic Alliance and the policy of co-operation. From this notion of ambition emerge both the host of difficulties concerning the Atlantic Alliance and the resolution to transform the policy of domination toward Africa into a policy of cooperation.

However, it will not do to hold an overly schematic view. Ideol-ogies exist, regimes exist, and this is what provokes certain difficul-ties in according priority to the nation-state. Regimes do exist. Dur-ing the war, from 1940–44, innumerable texts of General de Gaulle speak not only of Germany, but of Hitler's Germany. Since 1947, innumerable texts — vastly increased, moreover, recently — speak of the totalitarian regimes to the East. The great difference is that they are considered as having to be fought against as transitory entities that will evolve toward the norm of nation-states confront-ing one another without reference to ideologies.

The greatest difficulty for General de Gaulle, with his concept of the nation-state, is not to conceive of regimes and ideologies, but rather to conceive of a political entity distinct from and superior to the nation-state. In any case, he has a deep horror of all so-called supranational organisms, whether it be the general secretariat of the United Nations, or the general secretariat of NATO, or the Common Market Commission. His preference runs to a Directory of the major powers: five in the UN, three in NATO, two in Eu-rope, and one alone in France....

However, the problem of Europe is the most vexing. Can there be a "Europe" without a certain transcendence of the notion of nation-state, as it exists in the thinking of General de Gaulle? What sort of unity can be achieved in a mere conglomeration of nation-states? And at present, the principal difficulty in the dialogue between France and countries like Germany or Italy is that General de Gaulle tells his European partners: "You are bad Europeans because you want Europe without in the least knowing what you would do with it. What interest is there in building Europe if it is only to contribute to an Atlantic community dominated by the United States? Why bother passing through a European stage?"

And they respond: "But in order to achieve a Europe such as you desire, which would be a political entity, we must pass the stage of the nation-states France, Germany, Italy, that stand at the heart of your opposition to any notion of supranationality." We shall have occasion to return to this issue.

"Realpolitik"?

Is General de Gaulle a proponent of *Realpolitik?* What does the expression mean? That states (a familiar tune) are cold-blooded monsters preoccupied by considerations of power rather than by morality.

Force and Its Diplomatic Use. It is a fact that General de Gaulle not only believes in power, but in addition, being a general, he attributes a special importance to military power. But, to begin with, he holds to a sort of cynical conception of international confrontations. It is the sort of "deal" or "tit-for-tat" approach commonly and wrongly labeled "Machiavellianism." Thus, for instance, when de Gaulle negotiated with Stalin in 1944 and the question of the boundaries of Germany came up, the decisive argument advanced by de Gaulle in favor of the Oder-Neisse line was that this boundary would forever prevent an agreement between Germany and Poland. This represents what one might call at least a very realistic conception of international relations. We have seen that, as early as 1945, force was indispensable in dealing with the American ally. At times it failed, as in the Val d'Aosta incident.[9] At other times it succeeded, as in the Strasbourg episode. Force is indispensable. Good will is not enough. We are faced with a very general conception of the role of force in political affairs.

In the preface to his book *The Edge of the Sword* is the famous passage that one might be tempted to call the hymn to force:

> Is it possible to conceive of life without force? Only if children cease to be born, only if minds are sterilized, feelings frozen, men's

[9] President Truman, by stopping military assistance to France, prevented General de Gaulle from taking over this little Italian territory in the Alps, as in the Strasbourg incident, which we shall describe later.

needs anesthetized, only if the world is reduced to immobility, can it be banished. Otherwise, in some form or another, it will remain indispensable, for, without it, thought would have no driving power, action no strength. It is the prerequisite of movement and the midwife of progress. Whether as the bulwark of authority, the defender of thrones, the motive power of revolution, we owe to it, turn and turn about, both order and liberty. Force has watched over civilization in the cradle; force has ruled empires, and dug the grave of decadence; force gives laws to the peoples and controls their destinies.

And, Colonel de Gaulle adds, "It is true to say that the fighting spirit, the art of war, the virtues of the soldier are an integral part of man's inheritance."[10]

Consequently, there is a preoccupation with realism, a preoccupation with playing the role of a power in international relations. Out of this emerges a consequence that has been decisive in European politics during the last two years: the difficulty of conceiving of a style in international relations different from the traditional style of *Realpolitik,* the politics of power. The press conference of January 14, 1963, rejecting the British entry into the Common Market, was considered an offense by France's European partners much less because of the substance than because of the diplomatic procedure utilized. Members of a community do not behave in such a fashion.

The same is true of the Argoud episode.[11] In that case, pressure was brought to bear on the German government to protest officially. Non-official protests are overlooked, and hence the German government was constrained to have recourse to the procedures of traditional diplomacy, to *public* protest, while in the opinion of the German government, the new style in European relations should have removed the need for public protest and diplomatic notes in favor of friendly, private discussions.

[10] Charles de Gaulle, *The Edge of the Sword,* translated by Gerard Hopkins. New York: Criterion Books, 1960, pp. 9–10.

[11] A former colonel, Argoud, one of the chiefs of the terrorist OAS, was kidnapped in Munich, probably by the French secret service. He was then "found" in a Paris street, arrested, jailed, and tried for treason.

It must be noted, however, that *Realpolitik* has a limit. It applies to everyone except France. In describing his interview with President Truman, whom he finds to be a very mediocre man, de Gaulle explains that his welcome in the United States was very warm, not so much because he was General de Gaulle, but because of the ". . . extent of the city's extraordinary love of France."[12] I believe this is very important. All states are cold-blooded monsters, but *France is loved.* This is what justifies her receiving a special status, not entirely independent of her power, but despite her lack of power. It is better that she should be powerful. More powerful, she will be more typically France. But even though not powerful, she benefits from a capital of affection in the world that no other country possesses, because no other country is France.

The Intrusion of History. It is at this point that *Realpolitik* becomes tempered by what one might call the intrusion of history into the political conceptions of General de Gaulle. We encounter this phenomenon on several levels: to begin with the most evident, the history experienced by General de Gaulle himself. His anti-American attitudes are in large part attributable to the relations between de Gaulle and Roosevelt between 1940 and 1944. The determination not to see the French army integrated within an Atlantic army, it seems to me, can be amply explained by the Strasbourg episode of January, 1945. During the German offensive in the Ardennes, the population of Strasbourg would have experienced great suffering if the evacuation orders of General Eisenhower had been respected, if the integrated command, insensitive to such a detail, had not been blocked by de Gaulle's order to General de Lattre to refuse to follow Eisenhower's orders. The attitude toward the French population in Algeria — cold, to say the least — can be explained, at least in part, by the attitude of the French Algerians toward General de Gaulle from 1942 until the Liberation.

In the second place, there is the very traditional concept of struggles and wars. This is well expressed in a phrase from de Gaulle's *Mémoires:* when Germany was invaded by French troops in 1944–45, de Gaulle commissioned General de Lattre ". . . to conquer cities,

---

[12] *The Complete War Memoirs, op. cit.,* p. 913.

land and trophies. . . ."[13] The concept of trophies, of the flags that one captures, is really the most traditional in military history. At the same time, one notes the will to see geography frozen in its historic forms. In speaking of Germany beyond the Elbe, General de Gaulle speaks more willingly of Prussia or Saxony. To say the very least, Prussia and Saxony hardly exist any more. I add, nonetheless, that insofar as General de Gaulle is a master of the equivocal statement, it is perfectly possible that he employs this terminology because it obviates the need to speak of the "German Democratic Republic," "East Germany," or the "Soviet Occupation Zone." I nonetheless favor the first interpretation, since the expression "Prussia and Saxony" is found recurrently, from the meetings with Stalin to the press conferences of 1959–61.

The third aspect of the contribution of history is that it provides the ideological sources of his nationalism. Those sources are twofold, and I should like to emphasize this point.

General de Gaulle is at once heir to the Jacobin patriotism characteristic of the Left since the Revolution, and to the nationalism that has swept across a part of the French Right for a century. De Gaulle is the heir both of the Jacobins and Maurice Barrès and of the "Action Française" historian, Jacques Bainville. Hence, we see plainly that for General de Gaulle, the trip through Germany in 1962 marked the culmination of Jacques Bainville's *Histoire de deux peuples,* the coming to a head of a millennium of conflict. But in ending his press conference of January 31, 1964 by an allusion to the liberty, equality, and fraternity that France gave the universe 175 years ago, he was expressing the ideological expansionism of the French Revolution. One of the foundations of Gaullism consists precisely in its assuming the double heritage of Jacobin patriotism and the nationalism of the Right.

Another intrusion of history — the fourth aspect — lies in the conception of neighboring countries. We shall have occasion to return to this. Whether in reference to Germany, England, or Russia, no analysis of a situation is ever presented independently of what Great Britain, Germany, or Russia has represented forever, across

[13] *Ibid.,* p. 841.

the centuries. But at the same time, over against this intrusion of past history, there is a sort of *vision of future history*. It appears that during one of the rare interviews that General de Gaulle accorded to Marshal Juin after he became President of the Republic, the latter reproached him with seeing only what was in the distant past or what is in the distant future — and not what was before his eyes.

On the one hand, we find a man full of nostalgia for the past glory of France, with a very traditional conception of diplomacy and of power relationships. On the other hand, we see an outstanding capacity to look into the future; to see, even in 1959, what was later to happen in Sino-Soviet relations; to conceive (as we shall see later) of cooperation with the independent African state as a new form of an old French vocation.

The Man and His Style

General de Gaulle is himself perfectly aware of being an exceptional personage. This explains the well-known formula in his radio message during the putsch of 1960 in Algiers: "In the name of the legitimacy that I have incarnated for twenty years. . . ." But there is a great deal of deliberateness in this will to be an exception — an attitude described earlier in *The Edge of the Sword*. I have referred elsewhere to the passage on "character." I should like to emphasize another aspect here, namely, "prestige." Concerning character, de Gaulle noted: "A leader of this sort is distant, for there is never authority without prestige, nor prestige without distance." But, it appears especially in another passage where he wrote:

> First and foremost, there can be no prestige without mystery, for familiarity breeds contempt. All religions have their holy of holies, and no man is a hero to his valet. In the designs, the demeanor, and the mental operations of a leader there must always be a "something" which others cannot altogether fathom, which puzzles them, stirs them, and rivets their attention. In saying this I do not mean that he must shut himself away in an ivory tower, remote from, and inaccessible to, his subordinates. On

the contrary, if one is to influence men's minds, one must observe them carefully and make it clear that each has been marked out from among his fellows, but only on condition that this goes with a determination to give nothing away, to hold in reserve some piece of secret knowledge which may at any moment intervene, and the more effectively from being in the nature of a surprise. The latent faith of the masses will do the rest. Once the leader has been judged capable of adding the weight of his personality to the known factors of any situation, the ensuing hope and confidence will add immensely to the faith reposed in him.

And a bit further on:

Great leaders have always carefully stage-managed their effects. They have made of this a very special art, as Flaubert very well knew when, in *Salammbô,* he described the stimulus imparted to the vacillating troops by the calculated arrival of Hamilcar upon the scene. Every page of the *Commentaries* provides us with evidence of the studied manner in which Caesar moved and held himself in public. We know how much thought Napoleon gave to showing himself in such a manner as to impress his audience.[14]

Attaching so much importance to attitude poses the question of sincerity. I shall quote two texts from de Gaulle's memoirs — first, an entry into the crowd: "Among the delighted soldiers, the people weeping for joy, and de Gaulle standing at the center of the ceremony, passed that magical current activated by a great and mutual emotion."[15] But several pages earlier, he wrote: "Then, permitting myself to be caught up in a deliberate emotion. . . ."[16]

What do we recognize here? As a professor, when I use this word it surely contains no scorn — it is the *actor;* in other words, the man who experiences emotion and communion — for without this he would be a bad actor (or a bad professor), but maintains a great distance with regard to his own emotions — if not he would also be a very bad actor. It is impossible to distinguish in General

[14] De Gaulle, *The Edge of the Sword,* op. cit., pp. 58–59.
[15] *The Complete War Memoirs, op. cit.,* p. 956
[16] *Ibid.,* p. 813.

de Gaulle's behavior, sincerity — that is, deep conviction of what one says, as well as the reality of an emotion — from the calculated game — that is, consciously utilizing an emotion one feels as a conviction in order to obtain a political result. Sincerity and calculation are inextricably intertwined.

De Gaulle the actor, but also de Gaulle the exceptional man — the leader who is conscious of living his own biography. Ordinary men live their own lives. *General de Gaulle lives his biography.* This is extremely important; for to live one's biography means to behave according to what history will say. I am convinced, rightly or wrongly, that General de Gaulle does not know today when he will leave power. He would never accept being a physically declining President, for that would tarnish the image that history would hold of him, even if he were to remain in power until the end of his life. Better at that point to add a final prestige to the supreme prestige, that of Cincinnatus withdrawing when the *patrie* has been saved — Cincinnatus who would then write an additional volume of his *Mémoires.*

There is another aspect to General de Gaulle's personality that must not be underestimated. Like many Frenchmen, he is a man of letters, with all the good points and bad points that that entails. If you consult the German *Who's Who,* you will find that Adenauer lists the titles of all the doctorates *honoris causa* that he has received, and there must be close to thirty of them — from Swiss universities, fourteen American universities, Dutch universities, etc. The same is true of other German public officials. For the French, there is a general heading, "Distinctions." There is no such heading in the commentary on General de Gaulle. On the other hand, in the *Who's Who* listing on General de Gaulle, there is a heading entitled "Works," beginning with *Une mauvaise rencontre,* a play in verse, 1906 — written at the age of sixteen. This appears important to me as an element of explanation because General de Gaulle has a love of language — and he handles it admirably — and it also explains another characteristic of the man of letters — the inability to resist the pleasure of the *bon mot.* I am convinced that General de Gaulle did not believe for a minute in 1962 that the MRP would withdraw from the Government when he satirized the Europeans at a press conference by speaking of the common language and the international language called *volapück*. It was simply that the fact of having discovered volapück, buried since 1880, constituted a great intellectual pleasure. The taste for the *bon mot*, the love of the well-turned phrase takes on such proportions, moreover, that General de Gaulle has coined many new expressions, both in domestic and international politics — as proven by the number of words he has brought into fashion or returned to fashion.

The sense of biography and the sense of one's posture also carry with them a great source of justified popularity — the refusal of pettiness, the refusal of petty satisfactions. In *Le Maître de Santiago,* Montherlant has one of his characters say something like this: "In other times, people loved gold which led to power, which made it possible to undertake great things. Today, men love the power which leads to gold, which makes it possible to do little things."

In this sense, General de Gaulle is truly ambitious; and there are few ambitious men in French politics, if we define "ambition" as the will to act, and not merely the desire to profit from the advantages of power. This will to rise above the subordinate, it appears to me, emerges strikingly in a letter addressed by General de Gaulle to Edmond Michelet, then Minister of the Armies, on April 12, 1946. It was shortly after General de Gaulle's resignation, and the Minister had written him about his situation as a general in the army. Should he receive a promotion, etc.? Here are the words of his reply:

Mon cher Ministre,

In answer to your letter of the 8th, since June 18th, 1940 — the date on which I ceased to conform to a pattern and embarked on a fairly exceptional course — events have been such and on such a scale that it would be impossible to "regularize" a situation that is entirely without precedent.

Moreover no one apparently thought it necessary to change anything during the five years, seven months and three days of an epic struggle. Any "administrative solution" which might be applied today would be strange and even ridiculous.

The only proper course is to leave things as they are. Death
will take care of the difficulty in time, if there is a difficulty to
take care of.

*Veuillez croire, mon cher Michelet, à mes sentiments les
meilleurs.*[17]

Finally, whatever General de Gaulle's conception of politics,
whatever his means of proceeding, whether we criticize him or not,
he has replied in advance. In a chapter of his *Mémoires* entitled
"Departure," after analyzing the situation in 1945 following the
election of the Constituent Assembly, he wrote: "After the Assembly had elected Félix Gouin as its president, its next task was to
elect the President of the Government. Naturally I abstained
from submitting my candidacy or making any reference to my
eventual platform. They would take me as I was or not take me at
all."[18]

[17] *War Memoirs. Salvation (1944–46), Documents, op. cit.,* p. 384.
[18] *The Complete War Memoirs, op. cit.,* p. 979.

III

ALGERIA

Introduction: The Significance of
the Change in Regime

What is the significance of the change in regime in 1958?

As Seen from Outside. When General de Gaulle came to power, there was extreme concern in Bonn and in Washington, but fairly general satisfaction in London. Why? Because new situations almost always worry Bonn and Washington, and because General de Gaulle was considered a Germanophobe, hardly European in outlook, an Anglophile, who would very likely embark on a rapprochement with England. The error was in not realizing that the two primary objectives for de Gaulle were "status" and Africa — and linked to Africa, Algeria, considered both as a problem to resolve and as a curb on the two other problems: status and Africa. But England was felt to be a rival for status within the Atlantic Alliance and in Africa, whereas Germany was not. In any case, in order to pursue the two primary objectives, the Algerian affair had first to be set aside or eliminated.

29

The French People and the New Regime with Reference to Algeria. On September 28, 1958, approximately 80 per cent of those casting ballots voted "Yes" in the referendum to approve the new constitution (but the real meaning of the referendum was the approval of de Gaulle's return to power). At the time, there was much discussion over whether this was a "Defferre-Yes" or a "Bidault-Yes." That meant, then, a liberal "Yes" on Algeria or an *"Algérie Française-*Yes." I believe that even then the discussion made little sense, for what most characterized the Algerian affair was that it divided each Frenchman within himself. I will concede that certain French people were 99 per cent in favor of Algerian autonomy and 1 per cent in favor of French Algeria, while others were 99 per cent sympathetic to French Algeria and 1 per cent sympathetic to the political ideal of self-determination. But I believe that by far the majority of French people simultaneously held contradictory desires: that Algeria should remain French, and that a liberal solution — in the style of the right of peoples to self-determination — should be applied in Algeria.

To a lesser degree, the American situation in 1952 was not fundamentally different: people desired at once an end to the Korean War —"Bring the boys home" — and victory in Korea. In theory, this was contradictory. So Eisenhower was elected as the reasonable warrior who would resolve the contradiction. We might also see in the massive pro-Adenauer vote of 1957 in Germany the contradictory desires for European unification and German reunification. The two are incompatible. It was for one man to resolve the contradiction. I believe that the "Yes" vote in 1958 was primarily a vote of hope in the miracle, surrendering to one man the problem of reconciling contradictory desires.

De Gaulle and Algeria in 1958

Having completed these introductory remarks, I now come to the question: What was General de Gaulle's position on Algeria in 1958? To begin with, we must recall the mystery of 1955–58: General de Gaulle not only accepted the existence of rival political groups, each claiming to be faithful to him, but also encouraged from Colombey both liberals and antiliberals on decolonization issues. There were likewise the faithful Gaullists — some like Mr. Fouchet in one camp, others like Mr. Triboulet in the other. In the special case of Mr. Soustelle, when was he most fully Gaullist? As Mendès-France's envoy in Algiers or as the destroyer of the successive *Lois-cadres* in 1957?

Did General de Gaulle have precise ideas on how to deal with Algeria in 1958? To begin with, he would assess the situation empirically — "If I am there, it will be better by definition than without me, and I shall see what can be done concretely." This idea — "With me, there will be a state; and with a state, one can do the same things, but well, that others wanted to do, but would have done poorly because there was no state" — this argument was resorted to continually by General de Gaulle and Michel Debré, when they adopted the very same policies as the Fourth Republic on overseas territories or Europe. It is not the same thing, since it is being pursued by a France that has a state, whereas then it was being pursued by a France that had no state. . . .

Nonetheless, it is difficult to ascertain what General de Gaulle truly desired in 1958, because of his great talent for dissimulation. From 1958 on, General de Gaulle developed very highly the art of the deliberately ambiguous statement. Let us consider the meaning of the opening words of his speech in the Forum of Algiers on June 4, 1958: "I have understood you." (*"Je vous ai compris."*) In the mind of the crowd, that meant: "I agree with you." Now, this "I have understood you" *never* meant "I agree with you." It could have meant that, it could have been understood that way, but it could also have meant: "I understand you; but, this being said, I am going to lead you elsewhere." In the Algiers speech, one finds indications that point to a vision of the Algerian war and of the goal that must be sought, even through the dissimulation.

An incidental remark, but for me an important one: Was the dissimulation necessary? I have no certain reply. This is a moral and political question which is difficult to resolve, and which I cannot resolve. Would a straightforward statement of certain ineluctable truths earlier in the game have provoked the explosion and civil war? Would it, on the contrary, have appeased in advance resentments which grew all the more violent in that de Gaulle's dissimulation passed — and not without reason — for deceit? But how much dissimulation was involved?

In my opinion, General de Gaulle did not, from the beginning, desire the policy that he adopted in the end. There is nothing like having enemies for dramatizing your intentions! In my opinion, the vision of de Gaulle in Algeria developed by Maître Tixier-Vignancour in his pleading at the Salan trial does not in the least conform to reality, because it portrays a General de Gaulle knowing from the beginning, on May 13, 1958, where he wanted to go, how he wanted to get there, and proceeding precisely and methodically, almost without trial and error. Two points, however, appear certain to me. To begin with, as early as May-June, 1958, he had an idea of what the future of Algeria should be like: domination must disappear in order to arrive at a sort of internal autonomy. I refer you to the 1958 version of the Community: an Algeria occupying, as General de Gaulle was to say later, a particular place within the Community — that Community conceived as leaving defense, foreign relations, and other questions within the hands of the President of the Republic. A second certainty: in 1958, General de Gaulle was indeed French concerning overseas affairs — that is, as I pointed out apropos the Fourth Republic, *he did not succeed in distinguishing clearly between individual freedoms and equalities, and freedom and equality for a political community.* In other words, when he said in the Forum of Algiers: "There are only French citizens with full and equal rights," and when almost a year after his speech on self-determination, he assessed the record of what had been accomplished at his press conference on September 5, 1960, pointing to the fact that "complete equality of civil rights has been established in Algeria," we again encounter one of the two notions in the Preamble of 1946. Decolonization signifies the equality of individuals having the same rights as all French citizens — a notion continually confused with the right of peoples to self-determination. But, at the same time, there is a commitment to equality, in contrast to past policy in Algeria. As early as the Forum speech, de Gaulle was the first head of a French government since 1954 to speak of the causes of rebellion as other than a plot of a few irresponsible leaders or the influence of Moscow, to speak of the humiliations suffered by the Moslems for over a hundred years, to speak of dignity and the desire to erase inequalities. When he spoke of the "Peace of the Brave" to the FLN,[1] on October 23, 1958, it was received as a call for surrender, but the very label "Peace of the Brave" runs counter to what the leaders of the Fourth Republic had called the Algerian rebels. Similarly, there was a desire to overcome trickeries resorted to in the past. The instructions to General Salan prior to the referendum of 1958 stated: "The worst danger would be the drawing up of single lists favored by the official authorities." His illusion was probably then — and later, too — that elections in Algeria could at any time resemble normal Metropolitan elections.

Algeria and Other Foreign Policy Problems

Let us now attempt to consider the relationship of the Algerian question to other areas of French foreign policy between 1958–62.

The United Nations. The Fourth Republic's policy was continued. On the one hand, there was disdain and resistance to the UN because it involved itself in matters that did not concern it; but on the other hand, there was an effort to influence the positions of friendly countries so that the UN would not be too hostile. Partisans of French Algeria were reassured that certain statements and decisions were made not for themselves, but in order to satisfy the UN. In the "stew" following the self-determination speech of September 16, 1959, the comment "Leave all that to the UN" contributed to maintaining the ambiguity. The high point in hostile relations with the UN, however, concerned not Algeria, but Tunisia. That was to come at the time of the Bizerta crisis, in July, 1961. Partially because the President of the General Assembly, Mr. Mongi Slim, happened to be a Tunisian, the French Government

---

[1] *Translator's note:* The National Liberation Front — the organization behind the rebellion in Algeria.

and its representatives in Bizerta displayed great discourtesy toward Dag Hammarskjöld.

Morocco and Tunisia. The Algerian question continued to affect relations with Tunisia and Morocco, but less directly than under the Fourth Republic. At the outset, in 1958, relations between Paris and Rabat and Paris and Tunis were not bad — quite the opposite. During the summer of 1958, the transitional government of General de Gaulle accepted all the clauses of the Franco-Tunisian agreements (notably those concerning air bases) which had led to the fall of the Gaillard government. We encounter here a technique dear to the Fourth Republic: the new government immediately adopted the policy over which the previous government fell. The idea which emerged in 1958, or more exactly, which was taken up again, involved a North African solution to the Algerian problem. It seems that in exchanges with both Tunis and Rabat, the question was raised as to whether one day a North African ensemble might be created, within which Algeria would have a place. Unfortunately, there is a striking lack of documentation on this issue. As under the Fourth Republic, however, there was one major obstacle from the start: the Algerian Army of National Liberation had become a much more important military force than the Tunisian or Moroccan armies (or at least, such was the opinion at the time), and the Moroccans and Tunisians were not particularly enthusiastic about joining with their Algerian brothers in creating a united Maghreb.

Relations with Tunisia reached a sort of apogee on February 27, 1961, with the visit of Habib Bourguiba to Rambouillet. General de Gaulle listened at length, then made several oblique comments to the Tunisian President, who came away believing that he had convinced de Gaulle of the necessity that the Algerian affair be settled quickly. A few months later, however, between July 5 and 20, 1961, the Bizerta crisis broke out: shots were fired in Bizerta, blood was spilled. The responsibility of Tunisia was indeed involved, but the French retaliated with surprising violence. Tunisia referred the matter to the UN Security Council on July 20.

On the French side, it is difficult to ascertain what this "firmness" was intended to accomplish, since there was certainly no desire to remain permanently in Bizerta. On October 15, 1963, slightly more than two years after the bloody incidents of July, 1961, there was no longer a French soldier or sailor left in Bizerta. But in 1961, it was essential to fight in Bizerta because Bizerta was indispensable. Here we run into an aspect of Fifth Republic policy very reminiscent of the Fourth Republic style — an aspect that we will encounter again and again in Algerian policy. Why talk of "never," "inevitable," or "indispensable," when a short time later policy will reveal that such categorical statements were false.

Bizerta represents a particularly revealing precedent or example. Indeed, during the discussion of the budget for Algerian affairs in the National Assembly in December, 1963, when the Government declared that France would remain for a very long time at Mers-el-Kébir, the wave of skepticism swept even through the UNR benches!

The Community. The Community was at once the model for and the consequence of the Algerian affair. It is probably true that General de Gaulle saw in the constitution of the Community, 1958-style, a potential model for Algeria. Inversely, the acceleration of independence within the Community would have been inconceivable without the Algerian war. When the people of the Ivory Coast congratulate themselves in their national anthem for having achieved independence without violence, Algerians reply: "True enough, but because the Algerians resorted to violence, it eliminated the need for the people of the Ivory Coast to do so." There was a very tight interdependence between the acceleration of the political situation in Black Africa and developments in Algeria. African leaders tried on several occasions to serve as mediators in the Algerian affair. They never succeeded. One could make a long list of the trips to Paris, of the interviews with President Houphouët-Boigny and others. I do not believe that this ever, at any point, appreciably influenced the evolution of the Algerian situation.

Algeria and the Atlantic Alliance. We encounter here, as in policy toward Germany from 1947–50, a twofold and contradictory policy pursued simultaneously, or, at any rate, a new policy undertaken alongside the old. In October, 1960, more than a year after the self-determination speech, Mr. Paul Reynaud declared in a speech before the National Assembly: "It is not normal that we do not fulfill our commitments toward NATO under the guise that we are obliged to send our divisions to Algeria." Prime Minister Michel Debrè replied: "It is not possible to compare the state of our divisions in Germany and that of the allied divisions, and to pretend that we are betraying our European engagements. It is the state of our divisions in Algeria that must be compared with the forces of our allies. To submit that we are not defending the West in Algeria is to support the argument of our adversaries." This statement is based on the old argument: "It is through the Algerian war that we are faithful to the spirit of NATO, and it is up to the other Atlantic nations to support us in Algeria."

Now, parallel to this, another policy was outlined: tend toward self-determination and autonomy. This policy was in keeping with the nearly unanimous opinion within the Alliance, excluding Portugal: the communist threat did not lie, as the General Staff of Mr. Debré maintained, in reaching Europe through the South, whence the necessity of maintaining the Paris-Algiers-Brazzaville military axis. The danger was that the prolongation of the war threatened to throw the FLN more and more into the arms of the Soviet bloc and to contaminate the rest of North Africa, if not the rest of Africa. It is nearly certain that a few days before making his speech on self-determination on September 16, 1959, General de Gaulle had informed President Eisenhower of the major points of his self-determination policy, during Eisenhower's trip to Paris, September 2–4, 1959. That briefing must have satisfied Eisenhower as the major leader of the Atlantic Alliance. For him, Algerian policy, as it had been conducted from 1954–59, represented an element of breach, an element of danger for the Atlantic Alliance.

This is very likely what General Challe had not understood during the putsch of the generals that took place in Algiers in April, 1961, in defiance of official policy. At about the same time as the putsch occurred, the *Revue de Défense Nationale* published an article by General Challe that is extremely interesting in that he criticized rather severely the Atlantic and European policies of General de Gaulle. His reasoning appeared to run: "Since I am more European and more in favor of Atlantic integration than General de Gaulle, there is some chance that the Americans will support me."

Now, there was no doubt that, for the Americans, the policy of *"Algérie Française"* represented a much graver threat to the unity of NATO and to NATO policy than all the difficulties that General de Gaulle might create over the policy of Atlantic military integration and European integration. Anything was preferable to a defender of *Algérie Française.*

This is precisely why the solution of the Algerian impasse and the evolution towards independence brought about a sort of reestablishment of unity within the Atlantic Alliance until 1962. It is also, indeed, for this reason that American criticisms of General de Gaulle only really became violent after the independence of Algeria.

The Stages and the Method

Let us now turn to the stages and the method of the evolution.
Chronology. The point of departure in 1958 was the idea expressed in de Gaulle's speech in Algiers and in the October 23 speech on the "Peace of the Brave" — that if the FLN really could see what was in its interest, it would end hostilities and then all Algerians could participate in forming some vaguely unspecified kind of new Algeria. On September 19, 1958, however, at the same time as the Fifth Republic was proclaimed, the "Provisional Government of the Republic of Algeria" (GPRA) was established. Immediately, and in part because of the referendum scheduled for September 28, the FLN was transformed into the GPRA.

The hesitations of 1958–59 were in part eliminated by the speech of September 16, 1959, which envisioned two solutions: integration, which was labeled *"francisation";* and independence, which was labeled secession. Finally, there was a proposal which had no label in the speech, and which was subsequently referred to in commentaries as "association" — ". . . the government of Algerians by Algerians, backed up by French help and in close relationship with her, as regards the economy, education, defense, and foreign relations."[2] What are the implications of the words "in close relationship with"? A reading of the Charter of the Community in 1958 reveals the meaning behind the maintenance of French domination regarding the economy, defense, and foreign relations. There was a vision of limited internal autonomy, but interpretations remained very free and open.

January, 1960: the week of the "barricades" and General de Gaulle's two speeches to end the insurrection. On January 25 he made a statement which to my mind, even more than the *"Je vous ai compris,"* represents the epitome of equivocation. In his radio speech, General de Gaulle declared: "Our task, in uniting all the communities of strife-torn Algeria, is to assure the triumph of a solution that is French." This statement could mean either *"Algérie Française"* or "It is unworthy of France not to give independence to a dominated country." Both interpretations are perfectly feasible. For many of those manning the "barricades," a "solution that is French" very much resembled *"Algérie Française."*

On January 29, they were confirmed in that interpretation by another statement in a speech by General de Gaulle: "To lose Algeria . . . would be a disaster for us and for the West."[3] It is difficult not to interpret this in the same way as Debrè's reply to Paul Reynaud, quoted earlier. In the same speech on January 29, General de Gaulle likewise announced categorically that there would be no negotiations with the FLN. "That, I will not do."[4]

Then the final call: "Frenchmen of Algeria, how can you listen to the liars and conspirators who tell you that in granting a free choice to the Algerians, France and de Gaulle want to abandon you, to pull out of Algeria and hand it over to the rebellion!"[5] This was in January, 1960. Here again, it is difficult to interpret this statement

---

[2] French Embassy: Press and Information Division, *Major Addresses, Statements and Press Conferences of General Charles de Gaulle* (May 19, 1958–January 31, 1964), p. 55.
[3] *Ibid.,* p. 71.
[4] *Ibid.,* p. 72.
[5] *Ibid.,* p. 73.

in the light of what finally took place. It remains a moot question whether what finally happened was a willful policy, or whether General de Gaulle to some extent applied the celebrated principle: "Since events have taken things out of our hands, let us pretend to have planned on the events ourselves."

"No negotiations with the FLN," but as early as June 25–29, 1960, negotiations indeed took place in Melun — they produced no results and were not true negotiations.

On November 4, 1960, a speech was broadcast over radio and television, extremely interesting in that for the first time Algeria was presented as in the natural line of evolution of Tunisia, Morocco, and Black Africa — a speech in which General de Gaulle first spoke of the independence granted to Tunisia, Morocco, and Black Africa. Algeria remained; and at that point it was obvious to all that Algeria was an issue like Tunisia, Morocco, and Black Africa, and especially, that this was the case in the mind of General de Gaulle.

December 20 — a speech: the Algerians will take charge of their own affairs, and it is up to them to "found a State with its own Government, its own institutions, and its own laws."[6]

The first French referendum on Algeria took place on January 8, 1961: abstentions totaled 23 per cent, which was more or less average; 75.2 per cent voted "Yes," and 24.8 per cent voted "No." This was the decisive moment — the turning point paving the way for the mechanisms of the years 1961–62. Still, there were ups and downs in the negotiations: the negotiations at Évian were announced, then postponed for the first time on March 31 because the French Government did not want to negotiate with the FLN alone, and attempted to include in the negotiations the Algerian Nationalist Movement (MNA) of Messali Hadj.

From April 22–26, the so called "putsch of the generals" took place, and it might well be asked (one of the most interesting questions that future historians might raise) why, following the failure of the putsch, there was not a speed-up in events concerning Al-

[6] *Ibid.*, p. 105.

geria. There was, on the contrary, a slowdown. Personally, I am inclined to believe that this was due to General de Gaulle's determination to avoid drastic action, and to take care not to "break" the army's spirit. If any one policy was pursued from beginning to end, I believe it was the determination to *diminish* as much as possible the margin of opposition on both sides — those in favor of *Algérie Française* and those in favor of unconditional independence — to bring both wings together around a solution of "independence within interdependence," as Edgar Faure had said about France and Morocco in 1955. This desire to convince the great majority perhaps made it impossible, following the putsch of the generals, to take steps that would have avoided the development of the OAS ("Organisation de l'Armée Secrète" — the French terrorist organization) in 1961 and 1962.

The first negotiation took place in Évian: May 20–June 13, 1961. Failure.

There was another negotiation in Lugrin: July 20–28. Failure, because of the Sahara: Should it be a part of the independent Algeria?

On July 12 came a radio and television speech: "France agrees without any reservation that the Algerian populations [a more multiform phrase than the Algerian "people"] shall constitute a completely independent State."[7]

However, "we must negotiate, and notably with the FLN in particular." Finally, there were no negotiations with the FLN "in particular," but with the FLN *alone,* and these were the last negotiations in Évian in March, 1962.

There followed an interim period from March 19–31. In the referendum that took place on April 8, there were 24.4 per cent abstentions, and 90.6 per cent of those voting said "Yes." Until June 27, the OAS had its day; after that it was virtually finished in Algeria. The referendum on Algerian independence took place July 1. On October 8, 1962, Algeria entered the United Nations.

This brief chronology is intended simply to review the essential events.

[7] *Ibid.,* p. 137.

The Method and the Factions Involved. We now return to consider the method and the various factions involved. The most faithful Gaullists were certainly those put to the most severe test. When the UNR formed its first parliamentary group, the political declaration that the entire group was supposed to file before the National Assembly contained in one of its provisions the stated goal of "maintaining Algeria under French sovereignty." Then too, General de Gaulle made it rather difficult for his faithful followers to reinterpret his thinking. I say "reinterpret" because in 1961–62, we were spectators at the *a posteriori* reconstruction of General de Gaulle's policies since 1944. Hence, at the press conference on April 11, 1961, he declared: "Since Brazzaville, I have not ceased to affirm that the populations dependent on us should have the right to self-determination."[8] Now, the final text of the Brazzaville conference in 1966 stated that "any idea of autonomy, any possibility of evolution outside the French bloc, as well as the eventual, even far-off, constitution of self-government in the colonies, must be set aside." The myth of Brazzaville was followed by a new myth: "In 1947," General de Gaulle declared at the same press conference: "I approved of the Statute of Algeria."[9] Now, the violence of General de Gaulle's opposition to the Statute of Algeria (passed by Parliament in 1961 and making some progress toward giving the Moslems equality) was particularly noteworthy.

There was another characteristic: General de Gaulle's reluctance to receive the support of the nonfaithful. The successive attitudes of General de Gaulle on Algeria more and more came to resemble that of those who voted "No" in the referendum of 1958, and of a small fraction of those who voted "Yes." But General de Gaulle steadfastly refused their support, which was not forthcoming in any case. Thus, we arrive at the paradoxical situation of 1961–62, when the forces of order struck out against demonstrators (even killing some of them) for protesting against the enemies of the Government. This was due both to General de Gaulle's refusal to accept the support of those who opposed him on other grounds, and also to a more general confusion.

[8] *Ibid.,* p. 114.
[9] *Ibid.,* p. 114.

I should like to insist on the last point for a moment. On the whole, the clairvoyants so far as the Algerian situation was concerned were not numerous. Blindness took several forms, the most widespread in France being not to see the Algerian question as including decolonization, the rights of the Algerians, etc. — not to realize what was involved in the Algerian question. This blindness was powerfully developed and maintained by our scholarly books and by our major newspapers and periodicals. In an excellent article, the *Canard Enchaîné*[10] reproached Pierre Lazareff, editor-in-chief of *France-Soir,*[11] for his article in that paper expressing astonishment at the French people's ignorance of what was going on in Algeria. The *Canard* suggested that it was perhaps because *France-Soir* had never reported many events. The silence of the major press organs, for the reasons that I have already explained, combined with what we learned in textbooks on Algeria — or more precisely, what we did *not* learn in the textbooks on Algeria — contributed amply to this blindness.

The other blindness (but a rather minor one) was the idealization of the FLN. It considered France a decadent country, whose salvation could only come through the purity of the FLN, incarnation of wholesome force; and thus, to aid the FLN was to aid France. This was the attitude, for instance, of Simone de Beauvoir. But it must not be forgotten that the extremists of Algerian independence were amply encouraged over the years by the horrors that took place in Algeria. Of course, some of them reacted only to the horrors on one side. But for many of the French, the striking issue was the acts committed in the name of France, which were always denied (or more precisely, long denied) but later discovered with certitude to have taken place. . . .

Before the Court of Justice, at the time of the trial of the pro-*Algérie Françaiso* generals, a captain filed a deposition that confirmed in August, 1962 what certain people had written regarding Algeria since 1954: "I declare," stated Captain Estoup, "under

[10] French satirical weekly newspaper.
[11] Evening daily with the largest circulation of any French newspaper.

oath, that Godot [one of the accused officers], along with about a hundred other officers, received the order, at that time, to use torture to gather information. Do not ask me the details. I do not know the torments of the man who gave the order, but I do know the anguish of the man who executed it. For a young graduate of Saint-Cyr, all myths and illusions collapsed at that moment. Why wouldn't he have executed the order, since the goal was supposedly of unquestionable ultimate importance, and was represented as a sort of crusade? It was said that the end justifies the means, and that the victory of France depended on it, but this justification vanishes when the end is not attained."

(I note in passing that this is a curious interpretation of the justification of the means. One has the impression of a blot on one's honor because of failure.)

The Jeanson network of young Frenchmen helping the FLN, and the "121," intellectuals stating their approval of disobedience, cannot be explained without this kind of fact, not so much to sanction as to demonstrate that, ultimately, the most guilty, in my opinion, are neither the people in the Jeanson network, nor the future officers of the OAS, nor even those who practiced torture, but the majority of the French people who tranquilly set off on vacation. The tendency to place all blame *a posteriori* either on the Jeanson network, or on the officers who applied methods that were disapproved of — and perhaps not that much, moreover — is a facile solution, in that most of the French population continued to hope that it could duck all participation in solving a problem that it sought to avoid.

The Moral Record. When independence came, these different factions reacted in different ways. To begin with, a number of officers considered that since they had been deceived, and knowing full well that nothing could be saved (all the statements of the OAS that I have read seem to demonstrate that none of its leaders entertained the slightest illusion), the policy to pursue was to burn the ground behind them, to prevent any middle-range solution in order to prove that the catastrophe was inevitable. This was the reaction of those who felt that they had been deceived, or that they themselves had let down the Algerians who had placed confidence in them.

The pro-independence "ultras" grew disenchanted. The FLN, which had become the Algerian government, was not composed of saints and heroes possessed of all the virtues of Socrates and Themistocles. Curiously, one part of those who had fought hard for Algerian independence lost all interest in independent Algeria, because, obviously, the latter necessitated a different kind of effort. For instance, approval of a policy of aid to independent Algeria on the part of a government that one had despised would, if one were consistent, require protesting against events in independent Algeria just as one had protested against what had taken place in the name of France in Algeria prior to independence. Therefore, some of the former "ultras" avoided the Algerian issue completely — they no longer went there, nor were they even tempted to do so. But others, among the more farsighted, departed for Algeria in order to aid the young Algerian state.

What was the attitude of the bulk of the French population at the time of the Évian agreements? I believe that at that time, it was necessary to speak out in a way that only a minority did. The cause of the French populations in Algeria should have been pleaded well before Évian; this was extremely difficult during the period of the OAS. When Pierre Nora published *Les Français d'Algérie*,[12] I wrote a critique of his book, and my principal criticism concerned its date of publication. Most of what he wrote about the French in Algeria was probably true, but it should have been written at a time when a small amount of pressure could have brought about some change. To write such things about the vanquished was to grant a clear conscience too easily to the French people, who were prepared to consider the defeated French Algerians as of no importance.

It is for this reason that the task of the year 1961–62, for a number of those who had fought against the successive Algerian policies of successive governments, should have been to bring out the fact

[12] Julliard, 1961.

that all French political organizations and unions on the other side of the Mediterranean had supported the French populations in Algeria, and that, therefore, we had no right to consider the latter as the black sheep of the French community.

On the other hand, one might attempt to foresee a relatively favorable future at the time of the Évian agreements. Perhaps it is because I have been closely involved in Franco-German relations that an analogy has kept recurring to me since 1962: What are the two countries with which France maintains privileged relations today? Germany and Algeria. This comparison may scandalize some people. It may scandalize the victims of Naziism because the most barbarous aspects of the Algerian war still remained child's play when compared to Auschwitz. It may scandalize the *"pieds-noirs"*[13] because the groups dominating postwar Germany are not the same as those of Hitler's Germany, while those who initiated an atrocious war are in power in Algiers. But the Algerians might also be scandalized. Though the Federal Republic has indicted the executioners of Auschwitz, France after Évian has hardly repudiated those responsible for the razed *mechtas,* the summary executions, and the tortures that took place in Algeria.

In any case, it appears highly significant to me — and this may well be a cause for enthusiasm — that it is with the two countries with which we have shared a maximum of suffering that our relations are most privileged today. This is what might have been said at the time of the Évian agreements, while adding, as with Germany at the time of the Franco-German treaty in 1963, a word in praise of the eleventh-hour workers.

The major defect of French politics is that they consist in general not in a desire to pursue a policy, but in a desire to prove that one was right. Now, this is a totally sterile attitude. It matters little whether so and so — General de Gaulle, specifically — supported or fought against a given form of Algerian or German policy at a given moment, or if certain of those who support a given policy today were in favor of an opposite policy yesterday. What is impor-

[13] *Translator's note: "pieds-noirs"* (literally, "black feet") is the term used to refer to the French populations of Algeria.

tant is that a given policy be pursued. I realize that this calls for an ability not to reawaken old quarrels, provided that someone else does not reawaken them by assuming for himself a continuity that may not have existed. It necessitates the ability to transcend old quarrels, which requires effort, but I believe that it is an effort essential to the success of a policy.

We must examine, however, to what extent the policy pursued since Évian corresponds to the conceptions envisioned at the time the agreements were signed in March, 1962.

Évian and After

Let us begin by examining what was decided at Évian, and the substance of the texts.

The Texts. Who negotiated with whom?

This poses a first question. On the one hand, there was France, a sovereign state. When the text refers to "the two parties" (Article 2 of the cease-fire agreement), the other party named in the agreement was the FLN, which appeared this time as a party to a treaty, to an agreement signed with France. The FLN finally obtained the monopoly of representation that it had claimed for long years. The major text, the General Declaration, notes that discussions took place in Évian from March 7–18, 1962 between the government of the Republic and the FLN. One also finds the following: "The founding, following self-determination, of an independent and sovereign State appearing in conformity with the facts in Algeria. . . ." In other words, this time self-determination can only result in an independent state. "The cooperation of France and Algeria corresponding to the interests of both countries, the French government, together with the FLN, considers that the solution of the independence of Algeria in cooperation with France is that which corresponds to this situation." In other words, self-determination will be the ratification of an agreement between France and the FLN, accepting both independence — a major concession in comparison with the policy of September 16, 1959 — and cooperation — a minor concession on the part of the FLN, since it had never expressly stated that it did not desire it, but a more basic concession if it were intended to engage the future Algerian state.

Now we come to a point that seems important to me. The FLN assumed responsibility for the future Algerian state. That is to say, more or less, that self-determination would bring to power, in independent Algeria, the signatories of the Évian agreements, or their successors accepting their signatures. To obtain the guarantees given in the Évian agreement, it was in France's best interest to see the leaders of the FLN become the government of Algeria — which constituted the second aspect by virtue of which self-determination became simply ratification.

The Algerian state was to be totally independent: "The Algerian state will freely choose its own institutions, and the political and social regime that it judges most in conformity with its interests. On the international plane, it will define and apply the policy of its choice in full sovereignty."

Two comments on this important paragraph: on the one hand, the social regime would imply (if the state were to become socialist) a number of measures that would be incompatible with the guarantees given to owners of real property in Algeria. A subsequent paragraph, Article 12, stated: "Algeria will ensure, without any discrimination, the free and peaceful enjoyment of patrimonial rights acquired on its territory prior to self-determination. . . ." Either this paragraph makes no sense, or else the provision for the free determination of social regime makes no sense. Consequently, right from the start, there was a contradiction between the "social regime of its choice" and the guarantees given to industrialists and landowners.

On the international plane, there was scant provision for coordination; there was no provision at all for harmonizing foreign policies, and independent Algeria was empowered, from the very beginning, to pursue whatever policies it desired.

In the general declaration, there was also, of course, a definition of the future cooperation, founded on the presence of the French community in Algeria: "Algeria guarantees the interests of France, the rights acquired by individuals and legal persons under conditions established in the preceding declarations. In counterpart, France will grant Algeria cultural and technical assistance, and will contribute a privileged financial aid to its economic and social development." In other words, from the beginning, in the Évian agreements, cooperation was the counterpart of the status of the French populations in Algeria.

Cooperation and Socialism. When, mostly through the fault of the OAS, the French populations of Algeria departed, and again when, following the land nationalization decrees of the Algerian government in March, 1963, new departures took place, the reciprocity of the guarantees of cooperation no longer existed, and on this point, the Évian agreements were voided of all substance. Another justification for cooperation had to be found. The question of the social regime was one of the most difficult for the Algerian government itself, in the first place because, there as elsewhere, domestic and foreign policies were inextricably bound together.

In order to launch a program of economic development, and to initiate the changes that would lead the population out of its state of misery, the organization of the economy had to be transformed. In order to obtain foreign aid, particularly French aid, it was necessary not to make a complete break with the liberal economic system. The choice for the Algerian leaders was approximately as follows: without capital, no economic development; but to achieve the economic development that they considered indispensable to the establishment of a socialist system — the only system that they considered ultimately favorable to the whole population — structures would have to be transformed so radically that foreign capital would no longer have any interest in making investments. In other words, for the Algerian leaders, the choice lay between socialism with, as a possible consequence, a prolonged economic failure; or remaining under an economic regime that they considered neocolonialist, or at least little likely to give Algerians equal economic opportunities.

What was expected of France, with its largely liberal economy, was that it would aid, in spite of everything, a socialist experiment. It seemed that France alone could undertand this situation. General de Gaulle stated it at the beginning in fairly harsh words. While the war was still being fought, on at least two occasions, he brought up the idea that the Algerians had every interest in remaining on good terms with France, for no other country would willingly provide them with such massive and disinterested assistance.

At his press conference on September 5, 1960 he said: "Is it necessary or is it not for Algeria to change into a modern and prosperous country? If the answer is yes, which power can lend itself to this task, can cooperate to the degree and on the terms desired? Only one: France."[14]

Much ink was spilled over the phrase addressed to the United States and the Soviet Union at the press conference of April 11, 1961: "Some people say also, 'Either the Soviet Union or the United States — or both at once — would try to take France's place in the territories from which she withdrew.' My answer is: I wish both of them a lot of fun."[15] On the basis of this comment, it might be asked what was the goal of the aid provided? What was the purpose behind cooperation, once some tens of thousands of Frenchmen living in Algeria had departed? Naturally, there was a question of economic interest: there was the question of oil.

A second element must not be underestimated: one continues in order to continue. This explanation may appear to be little enlightening or logical, but it appears to me to be the essential explanation behind the continuing of aid both to Algeria and to Africa. Once begun, there is no reason to stop. Things are in place, the structures, the forms of financial aid, of technical assistance. One is there; there is no reason to stop.

In Algeria, another consideration certainly intervened: that was Cuba. I am convinced, without being able to prove it, that in the eyes of General de Gaulle the aid provided to Algeria serves as an example. Even if Ben Della had not come to the Château de Champs to meet the head of state on March 13, 1964; even if more Frenchmen had been dispossessed in Algeria, aid would have been maintained to show the Americans how a country can be prevented from

[14] *Major Addresses, Statements and Press Conferences* . . . , p. 90.
[15] *Ibid.,* p. 117.

shifting into the Soviet camp by not compelling it to declare itself to be non-socialist and "occidentophile" in its foreign policy. It was to some extent a demonstration to the United States of what it should have done in Cuba in order to prevent Castro from becoming communist.

Relations between French and Algerian officials have varied according to the men involved. I would generalize a little too much if I said that the military officials were more successful than the diplomats. But, during the months of crisis in 1962–63, the constructive aspects of Franco-Algerian policy came more from the Commander-in-Chief, General Brébisson and his group than from the French embassy in Algiers, which preferred to adopt immediately the traditional diplomatic tone in relations with the Algerian leaders, who preferred the more relaxed and less formal tone they could use with some of the young officers.

Nonetheless, the Algerian leaders' conception of policy towards France has beeen since 1962 and is more and more (except for Ben Bella's visit to the Château de Champs) an element of permanent discord. Quite rightly, French leaders complain not only of cooperation's unilateral aspect, but of the fact that the Algerian leaders consider that to require respect for engagements undertaken in good faith (the Évian agreements, etc.) is neo-colonialism. The Algerian leaders flee from diplomatic contact whenever a question of negotiation arises concerning an engagement that *they* are called upon to honor, but turn to diplomatic contact whenever an advantage or concession that they seek from France is in question. The manner in which the Algerian leaders have treated even the most kindly disposed Frenchmen, the manner in which they have dealt with economic development — as if decolonization must first proceed to the ruin of Algeria — such policies have not been formulated and are not pursued with the purpose of improving Franco-Algerian relations.

Some observers who went to Algeria remarked ironically that Ben Bella thought that Algeria should be an "under-developing country." In other words, he not only left the sectors neglected by the French administration in economic misery — notably the peasantry, despite the reforms undertaken — but in the name of socialism and doctrine, he also allowed businesses, skilled workers, and assets that were, according to all theories, necessary to Algeria's development, to leave that country. At the same time, the under-administration of Algeria, already very grave during the French domination, has taken on tragic proportions, with the result that the French negotiators can never be sure (and this is a thorny problem) that the decision made by an Algerian negotiator will be carried out in good faith. Nine times out of ten, the opposite is true: even with the best faith in the world, the Algerian minister cannot obtain obedience outside of Algiers because there is no response from the administrative apparatus.

Despite these difficulties, Franco-Algerian relations have not passed through any stages leading toward a break. The official visit of Ben Bella on March 13, 1964 marked, on the contrary, a new spirit of initiative. This was because, during that time, General de Gaulle was defining and putting into practice, in regard to Africa and the whole of the "third world," an over-all policy particularly pleasing to the Algerian government, in that the latter was hoping for a privileged position within that policy.

IV

FROM THE COMMUNITY
TO COOPERATION

The Contradictory Attempt of 1958

The Visit to Africa. General de Gaulle visited Madagascar and
Africa from August 20–29, 1958, and both in a premeditated fashion and at the urging of the African leaders and crowds, defined
the future policy of the Fifth Republic toward Africa. I should like
to recall in passing what I said about Algeria: there was a close
relationship between ideas and vocabulary concerning Africa, and
what was to become Algerian policy one year later. Already, in
Madagascar, on August 28, General de Gaulle employed the word
"secession" in speaking of independence, stating that the choice lay
between independence, seen as secession, and "a community on a
federal model, with separate domains and a common domain." This
was very clearly his aspiration concerning Algeria also.

On August 24, in Brazzaville, he declared: "Whoever desires
independence may have it immediately." A "No" vote in the refer-

endum[1] meant secession, but independence was not irrevocably surrendered in the event of a "Yes" vote: "Better still — if some territory within this community should in the long run, at the end of a specified time whose end I shall not stipulate, feel capable of exercising all the duties and obligations of independence, then it may decide through its elected assembly, and if necessary, through a referendum of its population, to become independent. After which, the Community will record its decision, and an agreement will regulate the conditions of transfer between the territory assuming its independence and following its own path, and the Community itself."

Finally, in Conakry, on August 26, there was another appeal for a "Yes" vote (but the answer in Guinea was to be "No!"). "France, I am sure, will participate in the Community with all the means at her disposal and despite her burdens, and as everyone knows, those burdens are heavy. . . ." Despite the burdens, there will be cooperation if there is a Community.

What was that Community in 1958?

The Constitution and Organic Laws. I should like to linger for a moment over the Constitution itself and the organic laws that followed it. Title 12 spoke of the Community, and we shall see that it referred to a federal system where everything depended on the President, who held all the powers.

Article 77: "In the Community instituted by the present Constitution, the States shall enjoy autonomy. They shall administer themselves and manage their own affairs democratically and freely." This meant internal autonomy.

Article 80: "The President of the Republic shall preside over and represent the Community." We shall see that the organs: Executive Council, Senate, and Court of Arbitration, were all dependent on the President. "The Executive Council of the Community shall be presided over by the President of the Community. It shall consist of

[1] Articles 77–87 of the French constitution of 1958 outlined the proposed French Community. A referendum was held on September 28, 1958 in both France and her African territories to approve this constitution.

the Premier of the Republic, the heads of Government of each of the member States of the Community, and the ministers responsible for the common affairs of the Community. The Executive Council shall organize the cooperation of members of the Community on the Government and administrative levels."

One incidental remark, here: if the Community failed, it was for reasons that we shall examine in a moment, but it was also because of the uncooperative behavior of high officials in many ministries in Paris. Why did they behave in an uncooperative fashion? . . . Because they were French, and being French, they possessed the centralizing state of mind of the Jacobins. In most of the ministries high officials are psychologically incapable of imagining, and thus of respecting, a decentralized system of decision making. The good regime is one in which they can make all the decisions in the name of others, and of course in their interest. How could French officials have adopted toward Africa an attitude other than that which they applied to local collectivities within France? French high officials did not even conceive of making collective decisions with African officials — not because they were Africans, but because decentralized and collegial decision making was unimaginable to them. Apart from all political developments, this factor contributed enormously to the Community system's failure.

It was Article 86 of the Constitution that posed the greatest problems: a member state of the Community could become independent, but it ceased then to belong to the Community. We shall see later that this had to be modified very quickly. But above all it was the organic laws that showed to what extent this Community was not community-minded, or more precisely, that it was a community only to the extent that everything was directed by the President. The ordinance of December 19, 1958 defining the organic law of the Executive Council stipulated: "The President shall establish the agenda of the meetings of the Executive Council. The Executive Council shall deliberate. . . ." Article 5: "The President shall formulate and give notice of the measures necessary to the management of common affairs. He shall supervise their execution." The Executive Council could deliberate, but it was the President who formulated and gave notice of the measures necessary to carry out their deliberations.

The Senate of the Community was purely consultative. It could make executory decisions only in domains where it had received a delegation of power from the legislative assemblies of the member states. It was never to receive such a delegation.

The Court of Arbitration was composed of "seven judges named for six years by the President of the Community." Thus, even the Court of Arbitration had the President as its sole source.

The President presided over everything, and this was supposed to provide compensation for the fundamental inequality. The Senate was composed, in accordance with the decision of February 9, 1959, of 248 members, apportioned as follows:

> France, 186; Senegal, 8; Central African Republic, 4; Congo, 3; Ivory Coast, 11; Dahomey, 6; Gabon, 3; Upper Volta, 12; Mauritania, 3; Madagascar, 17; Niger, 9; Sudan, 13; Chad, 9.

284 members: 186 representatives of France and 98 altogether from the rest of the member states. The least that can be said is that the Senate did not stand for equality among the member states of the Community. This system was very rapidly shattered. It was the last attempt to reconcile the former domination with the equality that was called for. Lip-service was paid to equality, for such was the direction of change, but in reality domination was maintained because the President of France also was President of the Community, and because in the Executive Council and the Senate, the French were in the majority.

The only condition under which the Community could have been maintained would have been to make it really egalitarian, but that was not possible, for it would have meant that in theory French policy could be determined by a majority of African states. I believe that most French people would have been horrified by that idea. This is what explains developments from 1958 on.

The Evolution of the Community

I shall discuss this subject only briefly, because there is an excellent short book on the topic.[2] This book traces in a hundred pages the political and legal evolution of the Community from 1958 to 1962. I shall outline a few of the major stages.

The first meeting of the Executive Council was held on February 3, 1959. The last meeting of the Executive Council took place on March 21, 1960, slightly more than a year later. In between, the Senate met for the first time on July 15, 1959. It was during 1959 that ex-French Africa reorganized itself. The Federation of Mali was formed on April 4, 1959 by the fusion of Sudan and Senegal. The Council of the Entente was formed on May 30, 1959 by the Ivory Coast, Niger, Dahomey, and Upper Volta. The year 1960 was destined to be important, in any case, because so many states became independent in the rest of Africa. Even if the French Community had been more of a community, it is difficult to imagine that the contagion of independence would not have spread from neighboring African states.

On June 1, 1960, the Council of the Entente demanded the possibility of independence without prior cooperation agreements: independence first, and then negotiations on cooperation. From June to November, 1960, there was a spate of proclamations of independence and admissions to the United Nations. The years 1961 and 1962 marked the period of cooperation agreements, both with the four states comprising the Council of the Entente, and with states with which there had been a falling out, such as the agreement of February 2, 1962 with Mali — "Mali" referring only to the former Sudan, since in August, 1960, the Federation of Mali had broken up. In 1963, there was a reconciliation with Guinea.

Note the successive stages: in 1959, the organization of the Community began in Africa; in 1960 the original Community was abandoned completely in favor of independence, and from 1961 on, cooperation agreements were signed and those who had left returned

[2] *Yves Guéna, Historique de la Communauté,* Paris Fayard, 1962.

to the fold. To arrive at this point, it was necessary to modify the Constitution, whether by legal means, or by less legal means. . . . Legally, on June 4, 1960, Article 86 was amended by the addition of paragraphs 2–5, particularly paragraph 3: "A member state of the Community can likewise become independent through a special agreement, without ceasing to belong to the Community." This was contrary to the original Article 86.

The Constitution was likewise modified simply by a letter: on March 16, 1961, Prime Minister Michel Debré wrote to the President of the Senate of the Community, Mr. Gaston Monnerville, who was also President of the French Senate, informing him that the mission of the senators of the Community was terminated. Following this letter, it may be said that the Senate of the Community no longer existed. Theoretically, a so-called renovated Community of seven still exists: the countries of the former French Equatorial Africa, Senegal, Madagascar, and France. But I believe that it is useless to belabor the issue, because this Community has never worked. In reality, what has existed is relations between France and the French-speaking African states, or groups of states when they are formed. I draw your attention to the substance of the agreements signed in 1961 — it is extremely interesting. To take just one or two examples: on July 15, 1960, an agreement was signed between France and Gabon. An exchange of letters following the agreement very closely resembled the exchanges of letters with Germany in 1952 and 1954. Independence is granted on the condition that the state agree, upon becoming independent, to respect the cooperation agreements signed previously. Two systems entered into operation simultaneously: independence and cooperation agreements. One did not function without the other.

Thus, on July 15, Mr. Debré wrote to Mr. Léon M'Ba, President of Gabon: "I should appreciate the favor of your acknowledging the arrival of this letter by a confirmation of the fact that, upon proclamation of the independence of the Republic of Gabon, the government of the Republic of Gabon will proceed to the signature of the cooperation agreements. . . . It goes without saying that the government of the French Republic will likewise do so."

Similar texts were signed with other countries after independence; for instance the agreement on cooperation in foreign policy signed between France and the Federation of Mali. What precise engagements does such a text provide for? None. Article 4: "The French government and the government of the Federation of Mali will keep each other mutually informed and will consult with each other concerning foreign policy problems." It amounted in fact to independence, with, however, the possibility proposed by the African states themselves (as in the case of Gabon) of calling on French troops in case of need, either through the government, or through their ambassador in Paris in case the government were prevented from doing so. The African states wanted independence, meaning, from the point of view of French political structures, to deal as much as possible with the Quai d'Orsay. Then they realized that this was rather bad for them, for to deal with the Quai d'Orsay meant to be treated exactly the same as all the other countries in the world. But then, what would become of cooperation; that is, of French aid? It was for this reason that the African states desired that a Ministry of Cooperation be created. But that posed a very serious structural problem: the channels of relations between Paris and the African states are various and involved.[3]

National Ambition versus Cartiérisme

Do the African countries really suffer as a result of structural disorders? . . . They both suffer and profit from them. They suffer from them in that they never know what door to knock on. They profit from them in that disorder keeps aid free of control. Those who talk of the need, for reasons of decolonization, to arrive at multilateralism, to put an end to Franco-African bilateralism — and there are both French and Africans among them — either forget (as the Africans do), or else ignore (as the French do) that bilateralism is a magnificent relationship. It makes it possible to ob-

[3] See the so-called Jeanneney Report: Ministère d'État chargé de la Réforme administrative, *La Politique de coopération avec les pays en voie de développement*, Imprimerie nationale, 1963, 2 vols.

tain aid without control, so that all the disorders denounced by the adversaries if French assistance to the African states still remain a shadow of the reality. Anecdotes recounting abuses in the aid program have one major drawback; they completely blur the debate between "Cartiérisme" and national ambition.

What is "Cartiérisme"? The critical articles by Raymond Cartier in *Paris-Match* are interesting in that they bring to mind a Molière comedy. I refer to the scene in *Le malade imaginaire* between Toinette and Argan. "France has not built enough houses: it is because of cooperation. Brittany is economically underprivileged: it is because of cooperation. Inflation threatens: it is because of cooperation." Cartier follows Molière even further, since Toinette explains to Argan that in order to have a strong right arm, one must cut off his left arm, and one can continue at length along these lines of reasoning in following Cartier.

Why the "Cartiérisme" of a magazine such as *Paris-Match?* One incidental remark: I wrote in a daily newspaper — and I believe that this shocked many of the newspaper's readers — that if the Weimar Republic had had an issue like cooperation, Hitler might not have needed antisemitism. Indeed, the intellectual process is the same. The great audience of a magazine like *Paris-Match* (the circulation is about one and a half million), is divided by all the problems that divide the French people. To study French economic difficulties as structures — posing for consideration, for instance, the issue of property — is to divide the readers; it is to provoke discontent. In order to explain that all the miseries that the various categories of readers complain about have one cause only, a scapegoat must be found outside the community of readers. This can be the Jews, or it can be cooperation. Cooperation is an admirable find to explain to the readers the sources of their discontents in various sectors, without dividing them against each other. They can remain perfectly content among themselves. I might add that *Paris-Match* has not been particularly consistent in proposing as the great heroes of recent years for their readers to admire men like Kennedy, de Gaulle, and John XXIII, all of whom fought in favor of cooperation, although for different motives.

For General de Gaulle, cooperation takes on an entirely different color. This was explained very clearly in his message to the Assemblée on December 11, 1962: "In order to resolve the world's greatest problem — the accession of all peoples to modern civilization — France can and must play a weighty role. She must know how to develop her economic, technical and cultural resources so as to lend widespread assistance to others, and her public authorities must be capable of applying a prolonged and orderly effort! How true this is, and above all for the African states, Algeria included, toward whom our historic vocation henceforth will take the form of cooperation!" I should like to emphasize particularly the adverb *henceforth*. Herein lies the major effect of gaullism applied to Africa: to win the acceptance of the French people for the idea that domination and cooperation are but different forms of one national ambition. The twentieth century requires that one no longer dominate, but cooperate — domination and cooperation both serving the cause of national ambition.

Then: "cooperation, in the name of what?" A first reply may be sought in the attitudes of the Africans themselves. France must cooperate because it is from her that aid is expected. It is extremely interesting to read a poll annexed to the Jeanneney Report, entitled *The Attitudes of Young Africans toward Foreign Aid*. Here we find the reasons, the prejudices behind the reasons why one country's presence is preferred over another; why the aid of one country is preferred over that of another; why it is rejected. For instance, Africans supposedly prefer the French for instruction and civilization because the French like the Africans. If they prefer the aid of the US, the USSR, or Germany, it is "because they are rich." Germany is rejected because of its past, the United States because of its racism, and the small number of those rejecting France do so on the basis of past exploitation.

However, this does not altogether suffice to justify French aid as a domestic political issue, and when French leaders have to justify the aid program, they are in general extremely uncomfortable. I believe that the best text on this subject prior to the Jeanneney Report was the press conference held by Mr. Foyer, then Minister of

Cooperation, on March 13, 1962. "The first reason is that the policy that we are pursuing is one of the means of *rayonnement* left open to France. The second reason is that, in any case, we have a responsibility before History." The *in any case* is interesting. As the Jeanneney Report implied, there are scarcely any economic arguments to justify our form of technical assistance and aid. Economic reasons would serve much more to justify German aid, for instance, in that the latter consists in profitable loans and investments much more than in technical assistance proper — the massive presence of teachers of all sorts and of administrators to get local administrations off the ground.

In reality, it seems to me, to plagiarize Bergson, that the two sole sources of morality and cooperation are what one might call "moralism" — whether Christian or the humanist type of the eighteenth century — and, on the other hand, nationalism. Since the first form was present among only an incredibly small number of French people (as among any other people), General de Gaulle made it possible, thanks to the other, to maintain the policy of cooperation. The first Christian or humanist motivation is accepted by only an infinitesimal minority of French people. For then, one would have to admit that the major solidarities are not national solidarities, and that the standard of living of the French must be brought into harmony with the standards of living of the rest of the world. Upon more detailed examination, the number of those accepting these ideas diminishes still more.

The nationalist aspect is represented both by General de Gaulle and by most of the antigaullists who favor cooperation. When it is said that "it is better to develop teachers for Africa than the *force de frappe*," this generally translates the desire to maintain a French presence in Africa. Why maintain a French presence? Because it is better than the presence of any other country, because the sole true culture that will be brought to Africa is the French culture (if not, it is no longer a true culture). I emphasize particularly this aspect of "cultural nationalism," which one encounters most often among the antigaullist partisans of cooperation. Between them and General de Gaulle, there is a divergence more on the means than on the purpose of cooperation, which is the presence of France in the world. I do not say that this is bad; I merely wish to point out that this is the basic inspiration behind the maintenance of foreign aid. It is here that the multilateralism recommended by the Jeanneney Report, and favored by many people, encounters a major obstacle: it would cut off the French partisans of cooperation from the major source of their arguments in favor of cooperation.

Beyond Africa

General de Gaulle has often spoken of Africa, but it would seem that, lately, there has been an enlargement of his thinking beyond Africa. This has taken place in two domains.

The first concerns the negotiations on world trade in Geneva. In the discussions on the "third world," all Gaullist policies aside, and all desire to play the role of spokesman aside, the French did act as spokesman for the countries of the "third world" on two basic questions.

In the first place, there was the struggle against the unrestricted liberal doctrine of the Americans. You will find this idea in the Jeanneney Report and its appendices. It is not true, for an under-developed country, that prosperity is born of free trade. On the contrary, they must benefit for a time from economic protectionism in order to give new industries chance to develop. Even for European countries, the liberalization of trade following the Second World War could only take place after a period of withdrawal, necessary for the restoration of order in economies drastically shaken by the war. Then, contrary to most liberal doctrines, it is only by very specific price guarantees that African or South American countries will achieve some degree of economic stability, making progress possible. I refer you to Appendix 19 of the Jeanneney Report, on the methods of price support for African or South American commodities.

Dear to General de Gaulle's heart is the very great desire to expand the policy of cooperation beyond Africa. When he stated in his press conference of January 31, 1964: "Cooperation is henceforth a major ambition of France," it was not the phrase in itself that was interesting, for it only restated an earlier theme; it was interesting that it came in response to a question on Latin America. Herein lies its novelty. The ambition behind cooperation is no longer limited to Algeria and French-speaking Africa, as in the declarations of previous years, but much more to all underdeveloped countries. Is this really something new? Yes and no. No, because you will find the same idea much earlier in a key text that has remained much overlooked: General de Gaulle's address to the United States Congress on April 25, 1960. There you will find all the elements involved in the present debate. General de Gaulle spoke of the necessity on the part of developed countries to come to the aid of all underdeveloped countries, without specifying that he had Africa in mind.

But there is another element that makes this a new policy. It was only at the end of 1963 and in 1964 that the General spoke so much of Asia, Latin America, etc., and one might inquire why. In my opinion, the explanation is simple, but others may well disagree: it lies in transferring the center of gravity politically toward Africa, Asia, and South America, after the nearly complete failure of General de Gaulle's European policy in 1963.

There was a shift in the emphasis because de Gaulle's European policy, which was intended as a means of winning independence toward the United States within the Atlantic Alliance, had failed. Another method was utilized to compel the United States to take account of France, and to cooperate with France. This was the shift toward Latin America and toward Asia.

V

FRANCO-GERMAN RELATIONS

Franco-German relations and European policy will be considered in two chapters, first, because Franco-German relations are interesting in themselves; second, because they are particularly important under the Fifth Republic. Of course, Franco-German relations, European policy, defense, Atlantic policy, and East-West relations are all closely related, which means that I shall often have occasion to comment, "We will consider such and such in another chapter, or in a different light. . . ."

Bilateral Relations

1958 and Afterward: The Relations Between de Gaulle and Adenauer. It might be said that the first contact between the Fifth Republic and the Federal Republic of Germany is contained in the 1958 Constitution. Indeed, the number of points in the Constitution of 1958 that were inspired by the Bonn Constitution, the Basic Law, is rather striking. Article 4 on political parties, Article 45 on the mixed commission, Article 32 on the duration of tenure in office of the President of the National Assembly, Article 54 on the constitutionality of international treaties, or Article 59 on electoral disputes, all appear to me to have been directly inspired by the German precedent of 1949. Only it was not in this form that the Franco-German contacts of the summer of 1958 came into public view. The spectacular meeting, with its even more spectacular conclusion, at Colombey-les-Deux-Églises on September 14, 1958, was the first encounter between General de Gaulle and Chancellor Adenauer.

What outcome might have been expected, *a priori,* in a meeting between these two men? They had many points in common; what were their outstanding differences? General de Gaulle is a general; Chancellor Adenauer has never donned a uniform, and it could hardly be said that military questions inspired particular enthusiasm on his part. General de Gaulle conceives of power as a charismatic leader; Adenauer — not by chance — even today when he is no longer chancellor, remains a member of parliament and president of a political party.

General de Gaulle has a taste for the impossible; Chancellor Adenauer, the most earthbound sense of realism. General de Gaulle has a sense of the tragic; Chancellor Adenauer has a horror of tragedy. General de Gaulle uses words which, on the tongue of any other Frenchman, would appear bombastic, and at times ridiculous. Chancellor Adenauer speaks the language of the chairman of the board of directors, with a veritable repulsion for the pathetic. They are both Roman Catholics, but the Catholicism of General de Gaulle is more Jansenist, more skeptical in regard to human nature than the more lighthearted Catholicism of Chancellor Adenauer, who is not any less skeptical in regard to human nature, but less like a hero of Montherlant.

However, despite these differences in character, despite the differences in their careers, at least two points drew them together: for one, the importance of foreign policy. For the Chancellor as for de Gaulle, foreign policy is the only true political arena. "The primacy of foreign policy" — the phrase was spoken in Germany well before the Fifth Republic in France. Second, both were statesmen; that is, they were not intellectuals, if by "intellectuals" we understand men capable of presenting brilliant running analyses, but incapable of holding to a firm line.

General de Gaulle and the Chancellor had a certain number of simple ideas regarding foreign policy, and they stuck to them despite all opposition, with a common horror of detail and a common taste, if not for history, where General de Gaulle moved about with much greater ease than the Chancellor, at least for global problems, with the details left to administrators. Hence, they met, they liked each other, and after several hours of meetings, it can be said that they formed a tie of friendship that has not failed to this day: General de Gaulle's affection for Chancellor Adenauer was largely a function of the Chancellor's admiration for the General. At the root of the relationship between the two men lay the kind of constant and faithful, and at times unbounded, admiration of the Chancellor for the General, and the General's satisfaction at inspiring such a sentiment in so extraordinary a man. In addition, they shared a fairly similar analysis of the international situation, which led them to pass over their very profound differences, to which I shall return. Firmness toward the East, the necessity of never making unilateral concessions, won common agreement easily, as early as the meeting at Colombey in 1958.

In addition, without being able to prove it in any way, I believe that as early as September 14, 1958, there was a sort of gentlemen's agreement between the General and the Chancellor — non-explicit, unsigned, undrafted, based on reciprocity: the Federal Republic would aid France in her Atlantic and European ambitions, and France would give firm support to the Eastern policies of the Federal Republic. On reunification and Berlin, France was never to take any initiatives that did not first emanate from Bonn. Since no initiatives ever emanated from Bonn in this domain, likewise none emanated from Paris. This theory was confirmed on December 31, 1963 at 8:30 P.M. in a single phrase spoken by General de Gaulle during his New Year's address. Indeed, in naming Pankow among the capitals of totalitarian states — totalitarian, but states — he was serving notice to Chancellor Erhard: "If you don't respect your promise of support in Atlantic policy, I can change my terms concerning the German problem." In my view, these simple words provided a sort of confirmation of the Adenauer-de Gaulle "deal" dating back to 1958.

Their personal relationship continued to be excellent, despite the misunderstanding at Rambouillet during the meetings on July 29, 1960, where it seems that the Chancellor agreed to positions on Europe that were not his own. He was severely reproached for this by both his party and the members of his government upon his return to Bonn. Even this did not affect the personal relations between de Gaulle and Adenauer: Adenauer is the only Head of Government to greet whom de Gaulle descended the steps in front of the Élysée Palace, an honor normally reserved to Heads of State. The apotheosis of the personal relations between de Gaulle and Adenauer came in 1962 with Adenauer's first official visit to France, or his first "state visit," as the Germans called it, on July 5–6, 1962; and then, especially, General de Gaulle's trip to Germany from September 4–9, 1962. Finally, on September 21 and 22, 1963, there was the farewell at Rambouillet. Before stepping down from the chancellorship, Adenauer paid a last visit to General de Gaulle in order to call attention to the particular importance that he attached to his personal relationship with the French Head of State.

De Gaulle and Germany. The Germans and de Gaulle. Behind this personal relationship, we must now inquire into the attitude of General de Gaulle toward the Germans, and of the Germans toward General de Gaulle.

As I mentioned at the end of the chapter on the Fourth Republic, General de Gaulle represents the third form of Franco-German rapprochement — after the initiatives of the pioneers of 1945 and the policy of the "Europeans" beginning in 1950. This third form symbolizes largely the rallying of French nationalism to the cause of Franco-German rapprochement — the two peoples that meet in the perspective of *L'Histoire de deux peuples* of Jacques Bainville: the Germans (*Germains*) and the Gauls. The trip to Germany is extremely interesting in that regard, for both the General's and the Germans' reactions. He excited the enthusiasm of the crowds

through his speeches, in the first place because he spoke their language — which was really a performance in Germany, despite the
fact that he had learned it at Saint-Cyr as the language of the enemy.
His diplomatic adviser, Pierre Maillard, an *agrégé* in German, could
coach him somewhat. The effort involved in memorizing his
speeches and then delivering them, as in France, with calculated
hesitations so that they appeared improvised, very much impressed
the Germans, as did his style.

One of de Gaulle's idiosyncrasies worked out in his favor in this
case. For he looks down, perhaps, upon men in general, but he
scorns no group or individual in particular; hence, in addressing
the workers in the Thyssen factories in Duisburg, he began his
speech with the word "Gentlemen." They reacted very enthusias-
tically to this because a Christian-Democratic leader would have
spoken to them condescendingly, and a Social-Democratic leader
demagogically. The style of simple human respect in General de
Gaulle's speech made more of an impression, on the whole, than
did its content; but the content of the speech in Duisburg is particularly interesting because of one sentence that goes very far in
explaining the over-all attitude of the French toward Germany:
"Today, what is happening in the Ruhr, what is being produced in
model factories such as these, no longer arouses in my country anything but sympathy and satisfaction." I believe that this statement
is a bit excessive, but reflects more or less aptly the reality, to the
extent that, as I explained at the end of the chapter on the Fourth
Republic, there has been a sharp change in French economic thinking: economic development in neighboring countries is no longer
seen as a threat to French economic development.

In the same address, speaking of himself in the third person, as
he often does, General de Gaulle stated: "For Charles de Gaulle
to be here, and for you to give him so cordial and moving a welcome,
confidence must indeed exist between our peoples." Here we encounter a personal element, a sort of inconsistency that is found both
in the domestic and in the foreign policy of General de Gaulle: is
he indispensable?

In domestic policy, here is the inconsistency: "The institutions are perfect and I am indispensable." If they are perfect as institutions, he is not indispensable. Regarding Franco-German relations: "They are excellent today because I am there. But my work is solid, and thus can endure without me." You will constantly find two notes: on the one hand, "It is because I am here," and on the other, "What I have done can now continue without me." The two themes appear in succession. In reality, of course, there is a change that appears with General de Gaulle's return. At the end of the Fourth Republic, when Prime Minister Félix Gaillard, for instance, or Prime Minister Bourgès-Maunoury, went to Bonn, the Chancellor was the grand statesman who spoke benevolently to them and delivered to them a sort of European "good-conduct" seal of approval. When General de Gaulle went to Cologne, the city of the Chancellor, he patted Adenauer cordially on the shoulder before the crowd, certifying to the Germans that their Chancellor was a good man; and reassured about its Chancellor, the crowd acclaimed both men. The result of the trip was so spectacular that even a weekly newsmagazine so profoundly anti-Gaullist, and fairly anti-French, as *Der Spiegel* was constrained to write: "De Gaulle came to Germany as President of the French, and he leaves as Emperor of Europe." Jokes were abundant in Germany at the time, such as: "Who will succeed Adenauer? . . . de Gaulle, and he will take up residence in Aachen!"[1]

Nonetheless, some statements and some turns of phrase or intonations in the speeches de Gaulle delivered in Germany provoked strong reservations, in the minds of both many Germans and a number of French observers. This was not so much because de Gaulle told the Germans: "You are a great people." In a sense it would have been better to give the Germans this sort of solidity and self-confidence back in 1945. But General de Gaulle cannot really be reproached for having only used this term in 1962, since he had spoken of the Germans as "a great people but one which perpetually holds out its hands to war" as early as December 21, 1944, in a speech before the Consultative Assembly in Paris. The

[1] *Translator's note:* Aachen, or Aix-la-Chapelle, was the seat of Charlemagne's Empire.

theme of the address in Germany in 1962 was rather: "a great people that no longer holds out its hands to war." But what he appealed to in Germany, and what he based Franco-German relations on, was less the political nature of Germany or the political nature of France, than it was Germany itself — whatever its political form, unless it were really extreme. But the statement: "We have torn each other apart for a hundred years" means, in effect, that the Second World War was of the same nature as the Franco-Prussian War and the First World War. This ran counter to the thinking of an appreciable number of German political educators, politicians, and teachers who had spent their time, since 1945, explaining to young Germans and to older Germans precisely that the war of 1939 was *not* the same as the traditional national wars, and that Hitlerism was an infinitely more tragic, more serious, and more criminal phenomenon than any other in contemporary European history. It was in this respect that General de Gaulle's speeches appeared, to many Germans, to run counter to the explanation of German history that they believed necessary to the development of democracy in Germany. Then there was the address before the Military Academy in Hamburg, where, restating a theme from a 1959 speech at the École Militaire in Paris, General de Gaulle declared: "It is a fact for the French and it is a fact for the Germans, that they have never realized anything great, either from a national point of view or from an international point of view, without, on both sides, a high degree of participation on the part of the military."

Said before the officers at the École Militaire in Paris, this might be appreciated; but in Germany, it aroused a good deal of conflicting emotion, for it was precisely such emphasis on the military in German history that first the Allies and then the Germans sought to combat after 1945. A few years earlier, at this same Military Academy in Hamburg, President Heuss had expressed exactly the opposite ideas, in pointing out that the task was to build a German society and a place for Germany in the world, where military considerations would count as little as possible. For this reason, there was a malaise in Franco-German relations, one that already existed before de Gaulle's visit, but that was aggravated by it. When former President Heuss made a private visit to Paris in March, 1960, and when President Lübke made an official visit in June, 1961, there was little evidence of this. Cordiality seemed complete. But in Germany more and more fears of a sort of contamination of nationalism were expressed. The principles underlying the foreign policy of the Fifth Republic were, to a large degree, principles that Germany had been striving to rid itself of since it had once again become a state. One must, nonetheless, be on guard against extreme judgments in this domain. Commentaries such as Nora Beloff's in *The General Says No* reveal the lack of understanding or the jealousy of the British. She sums up de Gaulle's visit to Germany as follows:

> When, at Munich, the General stretched out his long arms and said, in German but with a marked French accent [which was not true, moreover]: *"Sie sind ein grosses Volk!"* reporters agreed that they had not seen such explosions of enthusiasm since Hitler's day.[2]

Impartial witnesses agreed that there was nothing unhealthy about the enthusiasm. Miss Beloff's comments may be attributed to the rupture in the Brussels negotiations on British entry into the Common Market, which followed a short time later. But this type of commentary is also encountered among the ranks of the opposition within France, and this appears to me extraordinarily unwarranted.

The General's prestige in Germany was at its peak at the moment of his visit; it diminished subsequently. To the extent that polls are indicative, here are some figures. The population was polled on several occasions and asked the following question: "What is your attitude toward de Gaulle? Do you believe that, on the whole, his policies are favorable or unfavorable for us?"

August, 1962:

Mostly favorable	49%
Mostly unfavorable	11%
Undecided	40%

[2] Nora Beloff, *The General Says No,* Baltimore, Penguin Books, 1963, p. 156.

October, 1962 (after the visit):

           Mostly favorable 61%

           Mostly unfavorable 6%

           Undecided 33%

February–March, 1963 (after the rupture in Brussels):

           Mostly favorable 28%

           Mostly unfavorable 33%

           Undecided 39%

November, 1963:

           Mostly favorable 38%

           (a little higher, but not at the

           level of October, 1962)

           Mostly unfavorable 27%

           Undecided 35%

I should like to point out, parenthetically, that it is very rare to encounter oscillations of such amplitude over such a short period. But despite the fact that de Gaulle's popularity has waned, I do not believe that it is accurate to conclude, as Walter Lippmann does in his brief book *Western Unity and the Common Market,*[3] that the Franco-German binomial is merely a personal alliance between General de Gaulle and Dr. Adenauer.

The Franco-German Treaty. We shall see how unwarranted that conclusion is. But first, we must discuss the diplomatic culmination, the material triumph of Franco-German relations under Adenauer and de Gaulle: the Franco-German treaty of January 22, 1963. How did this come about? Upon de Gaulle's return to Paris on September 18, 1962, a French memorandum was sent to Bonn, proposing a procedure for bilateral consultation and a number of forms of cooperation in the domains of foreign policy, defense, education, and youth. There was a very positive reply from the Germans on November 8, and the process of formulating a protocol for signature was begun. But the protocol was transformed into a treaty in Paris on January 21 and 22, 1963. Who wanted a treaty? The reply is that it was not so much Adenauer, nor indeed de Gaulle, as the legal advisers of the German foreign ministry.

---

[3] Walter Lippmann, *Western Unity and the Common Market,* Boston, Little, Brown and Company, 1962.

Adenauer, wishing to give the text a somewhat solemn character, wanted a vote by Parliament, and the legal advisers explained to him that a protocol did not permit this procedure, and that under those circumstances, it would be necessary to conclude a treaty. So it was that what was intended to be a protocol became, instead, a treaty, which was drafted under rather uncommon conditions. The second or third secretaries found themselves commissioned to prepare a draft rapidly, which, for lack of time, was to be the final text — hence, there were a few inconsistencies, when compared with a regular treaty. I should like to analyze this treaty briefly, particularly because it is almost the only solemn diplomatic instrument signed under the Fifth Republic.

The treaty concerns "the organization and the principles of cooperation between the two states." One part deals with organization, and another with program. The part dealing with organization is based essentially on regular consultations at different levels: the ministers of foreign affairs, the French high commissioner for youth and sports, the German federal minister for the family and youth, the heads of the general staffs, the army ministers, etc. Consultations were to be held at regular intervals, the heads of state and government were to meet at least twice annually, and the ministers more frequently. The responsibility for coordinating the consultations in their entirety fell to an interministerial commission, presided over on each side by a high official from the foreign ministry. Those actually appointed were, for Germany, Dr. Joseph Jansen, Head of the Division of Political Affairs at the Ministry of Foreign Affairs in Bonn, and formerly a minister in Paris; and for France, François Seydoux, former ambassador to Bonn, and then ambassador to NATO headquarters in Paris. In practice, the ministers refused to be coordinated, and the task of coordination on the part of the coordinators rapidly became a fiction — all the more so in that no one knew exactly what was supposed to happen at each meeting. What *was* established was that there would be frequent meetings.

The part dealing with "program" was supposed to stipulate what was to be discussed during the meetings. But it was not always very explicit. Concerning foreign affairs, it stipulated that the two gov-

ernments would consult one another before any important decision
on foreign policy questions. The Germans subsequently deplored
the fact that the French government did not deem it necessary to
apply this paragraph before recognizing Communist China. The
word "China" was not mentioned in the treaty. But the important
problems on which there was supposed to be consultation were
listed as including East-West relations, and the Germans considered
that East-West relations were somewhat involved in the recognition
of Communist China. . . .

Concerning defense, the treaty was curious: "The objectives set
forth in this domain are as follows: in the field of strategy and tactics, the competent authorities in the two countries will seek to
harmonize their doctrines with a view to arriving at common conceptions." It was a treaty based on wishful thinking. In general, a
treaty establishes procedures or agreements; here, we find established the *desire* to arrive at agreement, which supposes that agreement did not exist at the time of signature. Once again, we shall
see that the margin of disagreement remained considerable.

Finally, concerning education and youth, there was provision for
a Franco-German Office of Youth, which was indeed created on July
5, 1963, during another visit of General de Gaulle to Bonn, where
a special agreement was signed by the foreign ministers. The Office
slowly began functioning during the winter of 1963–64. Its secretary-general, whose headquarters are in Bonn, is a French citizen: François Altmayer, former deportee, graduate of Saint-Cyr and
of the École Nationale d'Administration.

In the end, the Office was the treaty's most tangible realization.
Does this add up to very much or very little? The Office was the
culmination of a number of former accomplishments. In passing
judgment on it as an expression of Franco-German efforts, it seems
to me, several attitudes must be avoided. To begin with, there is the
issue of the so-called "last-minute workers" — which I also mentioned in connection with Algeria; and here, what must be avoided
is what has been called rightly the "veteran's" mentality. The fact
that a certain number of Fifth Republic leaders, at all levels, fought
violently in the past against what they advocate today is not a valid

reason for disparaging their accomplishments. What counts is that a path win acceptance, and that work be done. What is important is the accomplishment, and not who is responsible for it, or what his position was yesterday.

Conversely, one occasionally encounters among the ranks of the government and the majority party the erroneous assumption that Franco-German relations began on September 14, 1958. This is not true, and it creates malaise both in Germany and in France. However, consultations are so extensive today that, for instance, there is permanent consultation between the two majority parties. Even though the ideological equivalent of the CDU in France is the MRP, there are regular meetings between UNR leaders and leaders of the CDU.

Why, in the end, was there so little concrete follow-up to the Franco-German treaty? In the first place, because it was a culmination rather than a beginning — the crowning of efforts dating back to 1950, taken up and advanced by General de Gaulle. For Adenauer, it represented the culmination of fourteen years of effort to transform Franco-German relations completely. For de Gaulle, it must have been far less a question of a culmination than of an instrument of general policy — and it was to the extent to which Germans saw the treaty not as specifically Franco-German, but as an instrument of European and Atlantic policy, that it aroused much suspicion from the very beginning.

The Difficulties. We must now attempt to examine the difficulties in Franco-German relations since the Franco-German treaty. Officially, the only real direct difficulty was the Argoud incident. I have already mentioned this, and at this point I should like to explain why it provoked such strong reactions on the part of the Germans: first, because legality had been violated in a country that aspired to have faith in legality once again; and second, because such tactics were resorted to between friends. The Germans were extremely displeased over the abduction and General de Gaulle's systematic refusal to concede that there was anything warranting Franco-German discussions — not to mention his reliance on purely legal arguments, which was hardly customary in Franco-German relations.

Did Adenauer's retirement provoke a marked change in Franco-German relations? To begin with, there was of course a human change. From the point of view of psychological outlook and temperament, there are many more affinities between Erhard and President Johnson than between Erhard and General de Gaulle. It is hard to imagine the General at a barbecue at the LBJ ranch! Erhard does not share the taste of Adenauer, de Gaulle, or Kennedy for great historical considerations and for major issues of world politics. In addition, and this was true from 1961 on, there was a change in German foreign ministers. Von Brentano's place was taken over by a man whose ties are much more Anglo-American than French, both for religious reasons (Mr. Schroeder is Protestant) and for reasons of temperament and knowledge of languages. At the time of Schroeder's appointment in 1961, and even more, following the arrival of Chancellor Erhard on the scene in October, 1963, the question arose: Do we continue on the same basis?

In 1963 there was considerable tension, especially in the autumn, following Erhard's visit to the United States. At the same press conference where he mentioned Pankow, de Gaulle slipped in the suggestion that in 1963 steps had been taken "trying to place our relations with Germany on a new basis."[4] The words "trying to place" were already a sort of admission of failure in that they acknowledged that Franco-German relations were not satisfactory. Erhard's visit to Paris on February 14 and 15, 1964, however, cleared the air. Indeed, Erhard adopted a personal and interesting style: neither to be like Adenauer in systematically agreeing with the General, or in any case declaring publicly that there was agreement on all issues; nor to be like Schroeder, who thought that disagreement made cordiality difficult. On the contrary, cordiality must permit disagreements to be brought to light frankly. The result was that in 1964 relations between France and Germany were like those of a couple who, by dining together, sharing the same apartment, and doing errands together, hoped that they could finally overcome the fact

[4] French Embassy: Press and Information Division, *Major Addresses, Statements and Press Conferences of General Charles de Gaulle (May 19, 1958–January 31, 1964)*, p. 243.

that they were of different religions. The difference in religions is the attitude toward European and Atlantic problems.

France and Germany and International Problems

We shall consider these problems in detail in examining the European and Atlantic policies of General de Gaulle, while limiting our scope here to recalling briefly the positions of the two partners toward the East, toward Europe, and the Atlantic Alliance.

The East. For the Germans, the primary consideration in policy toward the East is the attitude toward the three German problems: the status of Berlin, the legal status of the German Democratic Republic, and the status of the Oder-Neisse line. In regard to the third point, General de Gaulle made the following statement at his press conference on March 25, 1959: "The reunification of the two parts into a single Germany which would be entirely free seems to us the normal destiny of the German people, provided they do not reopen the question of their present frontiers to the west, the east, the north and the south. . . ."[5] I have already indicated that in 1944, during his conversations with Stalin, de Gaulle had accepted the Oder-Neisse line. This press conference was a confirmation of that. It expressed, moreover, what the majority of the political leaders of the Western world think, without saying so. It did not imply that there should be recognition without any counter-concessions; it meant simply that the situation was irreversible. As for German unity, it is certain that in General de Gaulle's view, if Germany had not been divided, the European communities would not have come into being. In his view, traditional distinctions still hold today — hence, in speaking of the other Germany, he declared: "On the other hand, there is Prussia," implying the classic distinction peculiar to French intellectual history between the bad Germany, i.e., Prussia, and the good Germany, i.e., the Rhineland and Bavaria.

The refusal to make concessions to the East has been the stamp of French diplomacy since 1958, and in this we encounter a very appreciable difference between the Fourth Republic and the Fifth.

[5] *Ibid.*, p. 43.

The goal, the dream, and the hope of the Fourth Republic was always a détente and a summit conference. But General de Gaulle, who, as we shall see presently, has a number of reasons for drawing closer to Russia, has been much more intransigent than the governments of the Fourth Republic. Why? For two reasons, to my way of thinking. One is his refusal to yield without compensation. In the present state of affairs concerning Germany, any change in the status quo would amount to a unilateral concession on the part of the West; hence, we should not negotiate. The second reason is the necessity of supporting the Federal Republic in order to receive its support. But, on the other hand, there is a basic disagreement between Bonn and Paris over the nature of communism and the nature of the communist world. I shall return to this in discussing General de Gaulle's international outlook. For the time being, let me say briefly: in Germany, one often has the impression that Karl Marx was a Slav born in Nizhni-Novgorod, and that there is no cultural community of any kind between Eastern and Western Europe. The prevailing view in France is just the contrary. Similarly, the most widespread German analysis of the evolution of the Soviet bloc holds that there can be no evolution and that anything that is bad is bad once and for all. The reaction in France is very different, and we shall see to what extent French opinion supports de Gaulle on this point.

Europe and the Atlantic. Differences over Europe include the political and economic integration of Europe, the entry of Great Britain, and the goals of the European communities. Finally, the German position regarding the Atlantic Alliance is rather special.

German foreign policy was summed up in a formula by a leader of the opposition, Mr. Fritz Erler, during the debate at the time of Erhard's investiture: "No Europe without France, no European security without the United States." This means that if it is necessary to choose, security comes first. After the break with Great Britain, Mr. Alain Peyrefitte, Minister of Information, supposedly said (the statement was subsequently attributed to General de Gaulle) that "Great Britain was the United States' Trojan horse in Europe." The great failure of de Gaulle's European policy in 1963 was to have confused the horses: the United States' Trojan horse in Europe turned out to be the Federal Republic of Germany. This was true for two very simple reasons. The United States and Germany are the only two countries for which there is no problem posed by the issue of an Atlantic Community above and beyond the Atlantic Alliance alone. For the United States, this is true because it is the strongest country, and since 1949, there has never been any conflict between their national interest and the collective interest of the Alliance. For Germany, the notion of an Atlantic Community poses no problems because, on the one hand, their most immediate and evident national interest — defending the freedom of the two million Berliners — is a collective interest of the Alliance; and on the other hand, because most Germans have chosen Atlantic ideological solidarity over national solidarity: no reunification at all, rather than a reunification entailing the slightest risk of communist influence in a reunited Germany. In this, the Federal Republic is a special case, much more closely tied to the United States, linked more fundamentally than any other country in the Atlantic Alliance. This meant that any policy predicated on making Germany the stake in building a Europe distinct from, if not opposed to, the United States, was doomed in advance to failure.

It cannot be said, however, that General de Gaulle did not openly state his policies, and when Germans maintain that de Gaulle did not declare clearly what he desired (as a justification for German retreat), they have simply forgotten the General's first speech in Bonn, which is a remarkable summation of his global policy objectives. Here is what he proposed to the Germans, upon arrival, in reply to President Lübke's welcoming speech:

> Union — why union? To begin with, because we are together and directly threatened. Before the dominating ambition of the Soviets, France is aware of the immediate peril to her body and soul if, before her, Germany came to bow, and Germany is not unaware that her fate would be sealed were France to cease supporting her. Next, union because the alliance of the free world — in other words, the reciprocal commitment of Europe and America — can, in the long run, only conserve its assurance and

solidity if there exists on the old continent a bastion of power and prosperity of the same dimensions as the United States in the new world. Now, such a bastion could only be based on the solidarity of our two countries. Union, again, in the perspective of a détente, and then of international understanding permitting the whole of Europe (once the ambitions of domination of an outdated ideology have ceased to the East) to establish its balance, its peace, its development from the Atlantic to the Urals, with the imperative condition that a strong and alive European community be realized in the West — that is, essentially, a single Franco-German policy.

All the themes that we shall subsequently encounter are contained in this speech: notably, the idea that one of the goals of Western Europe is to be strong enough to unite somehow or other with a liberalized Eastern Europe to form One Europe that would be one of the major world powers, and that in order to realize this Europe, Franco-German union is essential. The deepest and most basic Franco-German divergence today concerns precisely the nature of Europe and of Atlantic unity.

VI

EUROPE

Economic Integration: "L'Europe Économique"

1958. How did the future of the European Communities appear in 1958? I believe that it would be useful to take as a point of departure Nora Beloff's appraisal of the situation, because it illustrates a confusing point. She explains that until 1958, the three major "Europeans" — Schuman, Adenauer, de Gasperi — did not want Great Britain to be admitted. Why? Because they were Roman Catholics:

> Their notion of "Europe," indeed, even though they championed the same political institutions and used the same supranational vocabulary, was never quite the same as Monnet's — though the outside world, and particularly the British, failed to perceive the difference.[1]

The last words strike me as true indeed: I feel that I clearly belong to the outside world that failed to perceive the basic difference between the policy of Robert Schuman and that of Jean Monnet!

---

[1] Nora Beloff, *The General Says No,* Baltimore, Penguin Books, 1963, p. 55.

Primarily their aim was to create a powerful superstate out of the
Catholic countries bordering the Rhine and the Alps. . . .[2]

What is the significance of such a comment? "Superstate" is a hor-
rible word for the English, and "Catholic" is even worse! Then, in
order to justify the English desire to enter the Common Market,
Monnet must *not* want a superstate or a Catholic union.

"Europe" in 1958 meant the Six, built on a Franco-German
foundation — the European Defense Community which miscarried,
the Common Market which came into being, but which could only
be realized after the French financial decisions of December 28,
1958. This is, of course, why the dialogue remains inconclusive:
the Gaullists were indeed opposed to the Common Market, but
when the Fourth Republic died, the Common Market was unwork-
able: it could not have functioned without the economic decisions
of the Fifth Republic. The polemic themes are plain.

The Emperor and the Pope. From 1958 to 1964, there were no
very fundamental differences concerning *l'Europe économique* between Paris and Brussels ("Brussels," meaning the Common Market
Commission). Nora Beloff comments:

> Looking back over the relationships between the Commission and
> France during the negotiations with Britain, a young German
> official suggested the analogy of the Pope and the Emperor: the
> Commission was the Pope, doctrinally defending the Treaty of
> Rome, and France was the Emperor, wielding temporal power
> against transgressors.[3]

As it turned out, indeed, on certain aspects of economic integration,
the Fifth Republic governments were closer to Brussels than could
have been expected of Fourth Republic governments. This was true
for a number of reasons. First, partly because of the circumstances,
partly because of the influence that men like Robert Marjolin came
to exercise on the President of the Commission, Walter Hallstein,
Brussels began thinking of economic forecasting — if not of flexible economic planning, in approximately the same forms and terminology as France. Next, the sharpest problem for the Common

[2] *Ibid.*
[3] *Ibid.,* p. 123.

Market since 1959 has been the issue of agriculture, where France stands in a very favorable position from the community's point of view, and where the Germans find themselves in the role of bad sports refusing to play by the rules of the game.

François Clerc sums this up well: "France wishes to export, but Germany and the Netherlands, who must import, have an interest in looking outside of France. The rapprochement of French and German prices threatens to lower appreciably the income of German farmers."[1] The two reasons are complementary: It is not in the interest of Germany to purchase her needed farm produce within the Common Market, and German farmers have no interest in seeing the common agricultural market realized — it would be in the interest of the consumers, but they are not much consulted on the issue. Hence, relations between France and Brussels have been facilitated considerably since 1959 by the predominance of the agricultural problem. In addition, the French negotiators proceeded very skilfully in explaining that in order to accept the entry of Great Britain, desired by France's partners, a number of decisions governing agricultural policy would have to be made.

The result was that a first group of accords on common agricultural policy was signed in Brussels on January 14, 1962. Certain of our partners still maintain today that we were dishonest — that our negotiators constantly insisted on concessions in agricultural matters in exchange for agreeing to the entry of Great Britain, the concessions were made, and the British entry was turned down. This explains the anger and the disappointment of Mr. Mansholt, Dutch Vice-President and a specialist in agricultural problems on the Hallstein Commission.

Next, there was the agreement of December 23, 1963. Once again, negotiations were bitter, and once again France sent especially competent representatives. I can only mention in passing the panic and terror provoked by the French civil servants trained at the École Nationale d'Administration among the Dutch, Belgian, and German negotiators. The French diplomats at the negotiations

[1] *Le Marché Commun Agricole,* Paris, Presses Universitaires de France, 1964, p. 43.

were either very experienced in economic affairs, like Olivier
Wormser from the Quai d'Orsay, or else had had training in economics that was quite superior to that of the English, German, or
Dutch diplomats. Hence, the French negotiators were clearly able
to dominate the discussions.

This was one element in the Brussels negotiations of December,
1963. The other was General de Gaulle's ultimatum strategy,
which consisted in announcing: "If we have not reached agreement
on a number of regulations concerning the common agricultural
market by midnight on December 31, this will be the end of the
Common Market." To which the others replied: "You can't do
that!" and Mr. Couve de Murville explained that we could indeed.
Finally, an agreement was signed on December 23. It was not put
off until December 31, because the foreign negotiators said to themselves: "Sign and get it over with — better to spend Christmas with
our families!"

This technique of negotiation was very similar to that used by
Mendès-France at the 1954 Geneva Conference on Vietnam: one
selects a date, and makes that date the critical element of diplomatic pressure — the twofold difference being that General de
Gaulle did not threaten to resign if the deadline was not respected,
and, too, in Geneva the pressure was used against adversaries and
not partners.

Success or Failure. Did this success in December, 1963 represent an over-all success in European economic policy? Does it not,
rather, upon closer inspection appear to have been a failure? At
Euratom, another European institution, there reigns a sort of chronic
malaise. This malaise was very evident in October, 1963 when
France voted against the budget of Euratom. This did not prevent
the budget from being adopted, however, since there is majority
rule. Why this malaise at Euratom? In the first place, because of
General de Gaulle's attitudes, as seen in his decision not to renew
the appointment of Euratom President Étienne Hirsch, whom he
considered too supranational — to replace him with Mr. Chatenet,
former Minister of the Interior in the Debré government. In reality, this malaise was the result of France's feeling that although

her five partners profited from the considerable advance that the work of the Commissariat à l'Énergie Atomique had given France since 1945, there was no perceptible counter-advantage to compensate for this opportunity given to the five others.

There was likewise little success in Brussels at the EEC — in the first place because most of the others were reluctant to advance into the real economic sphere. Painful compromises were arrived at in the domain of policy on energy because the others did not agree with the Commission. The basic ideas of the Commission, which were likewise those of the Coal and Steel Community, are found in the form of a memorandum drafted by a French citizen, who was Head of Energy in Luxemburg, Simon Nora — subsequently secretary-general of the Jeanneney Commission. This report on energy aimed at a coordination of policies, which France deems desirable, by means of flexible economic planning. The same holds true for the coordination of investments. In that domain, it is not the French who have held back. The others reply (and this was a great argument of the Dutch during 1963): "Why should we take steps toward the economic integration of Europe, on your terms, since, on the one hand, you do not desire political integration, and on the other hand, you have treated us with extreme rudeness in refusing to admit Great Britain!"

The result is that there appear to be certain economic obstacles to European unification today, and while France is certainly not solely responsible, the others reply that these economic barriers would not exist if France had not first blocked the way to political integration. This, together with my lack of knowledge, is the reason why I leave *l'Europe économique* now in order to turn to the question of political integration, or *l'Europe politique*.

Political Integration: "L'Europe Politique"

A Confused Situation. What is the picture of Europe today? I believe that it is fairly easy to sum up, but fairly difficult to understand in detail. The communiqué following the Erhard-Moro discussions on January 29, 1964, and General de Gaulle's press conference on

January 31 provide a clear picture of the conflict. The Erhard-
Moro communiqué reads: "Both governments are convinced that
the future Europe must be democratic, integrated, based on the Atlantic Alliance, and open to Great Britain." Forty-eight hours later,
General de Gaulle declared: "No European union, they say, unless
through integration under supranational leadership. No European
union, if England does not belong to it. No European union, without its being incorporated in an Atlantic community."[5] The "opponents" are certainly Erhard and Moro since, point by point, the
General rejected what appeared desirable to them....

But the reality is less simple, and we must pause to consider the
contradictions on all sides. In a word: regarding the future of Europe, everyone wants what he wants, and also its opposite.

If we draw a table of the positions of the various leaders on the
issues of admitting Great Britain, economic integration, and political integration, the results are eloquent. By economic integration,
or *l'Europe économique,* I do not mean only a common market —
the removal of existing barriers — but a true European Economic
Community; that is, over and beyond removing barriers and institut-
ing free trade, creating common policies, common decision-making
mechanisms, etc. By *"Europe politique,"* I mean a political Europe
governed by majority vote; i.e., having passed the stage of unanimous agreement between state governments. On the basis of these
three points, let us try to see *who wants what:*

Partners	British Entry	l'Europe économique	l'Europe politique
Monnet or Spaak	Yes	Yes	Yes
Erhard	Yes	No	Yes (weak)
General de Gaulle	No	Yes	No

Monnet and Spaak say "Yes" to all three points, knowing full
well that the entry of Great Britain would put off indefinitely both
l'Europe économique and *l'Europe politique.* Erhard says "Yes" to

[5] French Embassy: Press and Information Division, *Major Addresses, Statements and Press Conferences of General Charles de Gaulle (May 19, 1958–January 31, 1964),* p. 255.

the entry of Great Britain, a weak "Yes" to *l'Europe politique,* and "No" to *l'Europe économique,* to begin with because the latter evokes the specter of a protectionism at the outer borders of the Six that would cut Germany off from its most profitable trade; namely, with the countries of the European Free Trade Association, especially the Scandinavian countries; and in the second place, because there would probably be economic planning in such a Europe. Before the Council of Europe, Hallstein and Erhard took up swords, the one in favor of, and the other against a "planned" European economy.

General de Gaulle says "No" to the entry of the English, "Yes" to *l'Europe économique,* "No" to *l'Europe politique.* The task of the French negotiators in Brussels in January, 1963, was to refuse the entry of Great Britain in the name of an ideal vision of Europe that the French also denied. The dialogue was simple:

> We do not want the English because they would destroy European integration.
> Do you want that European integration?
> Positively not.

There are the contradictions. They are gradually being resolved on the antigaullist side, and in a most curious fashion. *Le Monde* reported an episode that took place in The Hague on March 4, 1964: Erhard arrived, conversed with Dutch officials; and the first version of their communiqué spoke of a democratic and *integrated* Europe; the final version simply spoke of a "united and democratic Europe" into which Great Britain should enter. The Dutch made their choice: better to have Great Britain and no integration than integration and no Great Britain. If I emphasize this point, it is because a number of General de Gaulle's political adversaries still act as if there were no problem, as if one could say simultaneously, "The British entry is indispensable," and "It is a crime not to favor political and economic integration," although the two propositions are contradictory.

Great Britain. Why did General de Gaulle take this position toward Great Britain? Was it really because the British would not

accept political and economic integration? Surely not. What is Great
Britain's position toward France? That depends. You know General
de Gaulle's celebrated formula: "Jealous in our days of prosperity,
benevolent in our hardships." It is an attitude of cooperation and
suspicion, where nothing is determined in advance, contrary to
what was believed in 1958.

There were at least two factors against the British entry into the
Common Market. The first was American pressure. There was so
much pressure in favor of Great Britain that it aroused distrust,
whence the idea of the "Trojan Horse," and it seems to me that this
was more spontaneous than calculated. In the second place, the presence of England would upset the Franco-German leadership, and
also, to some extent, the "gentlemen's agreement" that I mentioned
in connection with the relations between Adenauer and de Gaulle.
It seems, however, that in the beginning of 1962, the French had
resigned themselves to Great Britain's entry into the Common Market. Some employ the word "resignation." One day I brought up
the question with Couve de Murville, who replied: "We will have
no other choice" (*"On ne pourra pas faire autrement"*) — which
hardly demonstrates overwhelming enthusiasm.

For their part, the English made the same errors as the French
leaders in 1952 with the EDC treaty: they waited too long, and the
more time that passed, the less likely the British entry appeared,
principally because of Atlantic policy. This must be emphasized:
the major reason why de Gaulle rejected the British entry was probably not at all European, but Atlantic. There was a precedent for
this, which is too often overlooked: on September 24, 1958, the
General sent his famous memorandum to London and Washington,
proposing a sort of tripartite Directory for the Atlantic Alliance. At
that time, Anglo-French relations concerning the free-trade zone
were fairly good. But on November 14, 1958, at de Gaulle's request,
Jacques Soustelle, then Minister of Information, made an extremely
brutal statement, rejecting Maulding's plan for the free-trade zone;
and it appears that there was a relationship of cause and effect. Because there was no Anglo-American reply to the proposal concern-

ing the structure of the Atlantic Alliance, there would be no dealings with Great Britain on Europe.

The same phenomenon recurred in a more emphatic form at the end of 1962. Macmillan went to see de Gaulle at Rambouillet on December 15 and 16, 1962. They apparently spoke, as great statesmen often do between themselves, so vaguely that they did not understand one another. General de Gaulle manifestly remains convinced that Macmillan suggested that the price of Britain's entry into the Common Market was her contributing the British nuclear arsenal to Europe. In any case, Macmillan subsequently went to meet with President Kennedy in the Bahamas from December 18 to 21.

The misunderstandings were multiplied there. Macmillan was in a bad position in regard to British public opinion because of the American cancellation of the Skybolt missile program. Kennedy felt obliged not to let him depart empty-handed, and they improvised the Multilateral Force proposal. Although it really was an improvisation, it was presented as a very important accomplishment. So well was it presented, indeed, that General de Gaulle concluded that so important a proposal could not have been improvised, and consequently, that Macmillan must have known at Rambouillet that not only would he not give the British atomic force as a dowry to Europe, but that American control over the British force would be increased. I remain convinced that the decision to break off negotiations abruptly was largely made on the basis of the Bahamas meeting, more than European economic considerations. This may be likened to the classic bourgeois marriage: no dowry, no wedding.

What was a bit absurd was to have let negotiations advance so far. England was to prove this and then that, and finally the answer was "No," just when the economic negotiations were reaching a fruitful conclusion. Moreover, this part explains why de Gaulle broke off negotiations so abruptly. It was doubtless because time was passing, and there was a possibility that the negotiators would reach agreement on agricultural and economic questions, while the real divergence lay elsewhere. Of course, what offended France's partners was de Gaulle's style. What offended the British may be summed up in an anecdote which Nora Beloff attributes to a French official:

> Two neighboring farmers wanted to marry off their son and daughter. The courtship had been going on for some time without results when the boy's family intervened to ask him to make up his mind. He said he could not decide until he had seen her without her clothes on. Aghast, the two families consulted and finally arranged that he should look through the keyhole while she was taking her bath. The ordeal lasted for some time while the families waited downstairs. Finally the boy came down: "No," he said, "I never like girls with blue eyes."[6]

I believe that this gives a very good picture of the British reaction to the failure in Brussels. "If it was really for *a priori* reasons that the General said 'No,' it was hardly worth making us negotiate for hours and hours, weeks and months, on economic questions."

Europe for What? In reality, the divergence of opinion with Great Britain applies likewise to most of France's partners in the European communities. The problem can be summed up in the question: "Europe for what?" On this score, General de Gaulle is in a rather advantageous position. The others object to de Gaulle: "Why do you claim on the one hand that you want to build Europe and that this Europe would be a major means to your over-all political goals, when, on the other hand, you claim that traditional nation-states must remain?" The General replies with another question: "But after all, why do *you* want Europe? You have no motive for wanting it if you don't want it the way I do."

Concerning the "third world" of poor and underdeveloped countries, there is some agreement among the Europeans, although few among them desire, as systematically as France, that European policy be directed toward aiding the third world as a major priority. For instance, both at the Geneva trade negotiations and at the negotiations in Brussels between the Common Market and the African countries, it was the French who pressed for linking the Eu-

---

[6] Nora Beloff, *The General Says No, op. cit.,* p. 164.

ropean agricultural problem to the problems of the third world. Former Minister of Agriculture Edgar Pisani developed this idea in an excellent article:

> If we do not think of the problem of the flow of surpluses toward those who hunger, we shall be forced, with our backs against the wall, to turn to our peasants in order to prevent them from producing according to the quality of their soil and following their own talents. For so long as there are hungry men in the world, I shall refuse to propose such a solution to the farmers of France and of Europe.[7]

In other words, the problem of defining European policy on agricultural questions is tied to aid to the third world.

Second, the problem of defense. De Gaulle has sometimes said, "Europe will be made through its defense." We shall see the possible implications of this statement in considering the French nuclear force, the *force de frappe*.

But what is the true goal of Europe in Gaullist policy, and to what extent can de Gaulle reproach others on this issue? Three texts are particularly revealing: General de Gaulle's toast at the reception at the Élysée in honor of President Segni, Saragat's speech the following day to the Parisian press, and finally, Pompidou's statements on February 24, 1964 before the American Club.

In toasting President Segni, de Gaulle declared: "The question remains whether or not Europe will be able to rise into a coherent and active reality — whether or not she will establish for herself her goals, her attitude, her pace, that is, to define her own policies; her means of defense, and the functioning of her alliances, that is, her security; the contribution of her economy, her techniques, and her assets, that is, her aid to so many countries of Latin America, Africa and Asia." Thus, the goal of Europe is to define policies and build up a defense of her own. Before the French and foreign press, Saragat declared: "For Rome, as for Paris, the Atlantic Alliance constitutes an element essential to the defense of the free

[7] "L'Organisation mondiale des marchés agricoles" ("The Worldwide Organization of Agricultural Markets"), *Revue de Défense Nationale*, August-September, 1961.

world. Italy hopes that the Alliance will be gradually transformed into an Atlantic community." De Gaulle's reply would be, in substance, "But then, why do you need Europe? Why have an Atlantic community? Do you need the intermediary stage of European union?" For de Gaulle, the Atlantic Community could never be anything other than a dependency of the United States.

Finally, we encounter rather curious turns of phrase, such as Pompidou's statement: "Something new has occurred within the Western bloc. The countries of Europe have regained their strength and their economic prosperity, and certain of them have regained their self-awareness." (*"Certains"* is in the plural, but the context reveals that it should be in the singular.) "The old partition into two monolithic groups is outmoded. It is here that we see the role of France, whose geography and history condemn her to play the role of Europe." If these words say what they mean, and unless there is some mistake (but the "mistake" corresponds so closely to General de Gaulle's policies that it would be too fortuitous), this does *not* mean "France must play *a* role in Europe," nor "France must play the European card," but indeed "France must play *the* role of Europe because the other European countries have not yet become aware of that role." I believe that this, precisely, is the most important aspect of de Gaulle's European policy today: he will define European policy, while biding time until the others realize what it should be. I believe that there is a very deep conflict at issue here, in that General de Gaulle is convinced that he is playing what ought to be Europe's role, even though his five European partners are in fundamental disagreement with him.

A Varied Record. This brings us to our final point — an attempt to appraise the record of this policy of European union. I regret to have to quote General de Gaulle once again, but he must be rendered this one justice — no one puts his policies into words better than he himself! I believe that the occasion on which he best formulated his European policy was his press conference on May 15, 1962. He spoke of the complementary geographic, strategic, economic, and cultural character of "the peoples of this part of the old continent."[8] I emphasize not the words "old continent," but "this part of the old continent." In General de Gaulle's perspective, Europe extends to the Urals, and it happens that it is divided today. We are in one part of Europe; Western Europe is not the same as the whole of Europe.

The Treaty of Rome, the French economic and financial recovery: "In the French view, this economic construction is not enough. . . . Western Europe must form itself politically. . . . What is it that France is proposing to her five partners? . . . To organize ourselves politically, let us begin at the beginning. Let us organize our cooperation, let our Heads of State or of Government meet periodically. . . . Let us set up a political commission, a defense commission, and cultural commission, just as we have already formed an economic commission in Brussels which studies common questions and prepares the decision of the six Governments. . . . [Then, there will be an assembly.] After we have tried it, we shall see, in three years time, what we can do to strengthen our ties. . . ."[9]

Several comments. There was the episode of the Fouchet commission, charged with the preparation of a political community. They eventually reached an agreement, but General de Gaulle thought he could act with his foreign interlocutors in the same way as he would with his ministers: to change just a few words or phrases in the agreement made by the Six, saying that they were not very important. At which point, not finding the original text, the five others decided that the whole affair was no longer worth discussing. But what is important is, on the one hand, that the notion of cooperation and concert contained in the Franco-German treaty was considered as an example to be followed in European policy, although, in the meantime, General de Gaulle decided that the Franco-German treaty should be as bilateral as possible in its application, and should exclude the other Europeans. This kind of consultation appeared totally insufficient to the others. Moreover, there

[8] *Major Addresses, Statements and Press Conferences of General Charles de Gaulle, op. cit.*, pp. 173—174.
[9] *Ibid.*, pp. 174—175.

was the idea that the Hallstein Commission in Brussels was not even the forerunner of a supranational authority. Here, we come up against a chronic, deep, and insurmountable misunderstanding regarding what a transnational or supranational institution is. This was particularly noticeable at de Gaulle's press conference on January 31, 1964.

At this press conference, General de Gaulle wished to please the Hallstein Commission, which had, in reality, served as an arbitrator in the agricultural negotiations during December, 1963. He wished to please the Hallstein Commission, and at the same time to emphasize his rejection of supranational organizations:

> As always the elements of a solution were formulated by the technicians. But then, to reach a conclusion, the decisions, despite all the contradictory interests, could only come from the States. That is indeed what happened.
>
> The Brussels Commission having objectively accomplished work of great value, and offering the negotiators, as they debated, carefully studied suggestions, the governments nonetheless found themselves obliged to take decisive steps and assume their responsibilities. . . . However important the work and the counsels of the Brussels Commission have been and must continue to be, we have seen clearly that the executive power and duty belongs to the governments alone. Thus, once again, is evidenced the tendencious impropriety of concept and phraseology by means of which a certain parlance entitles "executive" a meeting, however qualified it may be, of international experts.[10]

Now if you look at the Common Market treaty (without mentioning the Coal and Steel treaty) the High Authority in Luxemburg and the Commission in Brussels are anything but a meeting of international experts. On this point, de Gaulle's attitude poses an insurmountable obstacle, although, at many other points, one might say that it is the other partners who throw words about. What, for instance, did the Germans do during the coal crisis of 1963? Apply the decisions of the High Authority in Luxemburg? Ask the High Authority to intervene? No — they applied well-

[10] *Ibid.*, p. 253.

worn, classic, national, protectionist solutions that had been applied for a hundred years: they raised tariffs on the importing of oil, they took measures of protection against foreign coal, and so forth. It is a fact that where problems such as agriculture are involved, no transnational executive is in a position today to enforce decisions of sacrifice upon peasants, on a national level. This can only be done by governments, and under very difficult conditions. Consequently, the prospect of establishing a true executive is much further from realization than European integrationists hope.

It is for this reason that we must introduce the difficult notion of realism — there is, it seems to me, a fairly appreciable contradiction of General de Gaulle's attitudes regarding Europe. He claims to be a realist. "Since there are states, we must continue with states." But to say that is obviously to block the evolution leading to a day when we can do without national states in their present form. In the name of realism, one freezes the situation. When he was in London in 1940, or dealing with Eisenhower or Strasbourg in January, 1945, General de Gaulle considered that *will* was stronger than reality. In his European policy, he believes that wisdom lies in submitting one's will to the reality of states. Obviously, one forms the impression that this realism, or submission to reality, is only applied because of his strong conviction that the reality is good, that the reality of states in Europe is a satisfactory reality in the perspective of his whole view of international relations, even though his speeches and writings occasionally suggest a Europe that would be a sort of nation-state in its own right. It is relatively easy to weigh the pros and cons of de Gaulle's attitudes. But it is much more difficult to assess the political record — so difficult that the Fifth Republic itself is at somewhat of a loss when it is called upon to do so.

In a brochure published by the government entitled *La Ve République a cinq ans,* there is a passage devoted to Europe. The least that can be said is that the passage is brief: "France has played a decisive role in European economic construction; she has contributed actively to carrying out the Treaty of Rome, both by the acceleration of the industrial Common Market and by the progressive realization of the agricultural Common Market. She has demonstrated her commitment to the political union of Europe in sealing the Franco-German reconciliation by a treaty of cooperation between the two countries." It is hardly possible to say more, for despite the repeated rumors of a *relance,* or relaunching, in the near future, the realization of a politically united Europe appears very solidly blocked.

Relations with Great Britain depend in part on who is in power in London. But in any case, British enthusiasm concerning the Common Market has dwindled — especially since the rate of development and growth in Great Britain and the United States surpassed that of the European countries in 1963. It was precisely the rapid economic growth of the Six that inspired the British decision to apply for membership. Is General de Gaulle responsible for slowing down this development? He has been accused of having contributed to the disintegration of Europe. I believe that this is true at least in regard to style, notably the brutality of his pronouncement of January 14, 1963. But at bottom, I have not succeeded in finding any "Europeans" today who define very clearly what they mean by "Europe." This is particularly true in regard to defense, to atomic power, to policy toward the United States, to supranationality, to the geographic boundaries of this Europe. General de Gaulle, for his part, has made his choices. Europe is no longer a goal, but one of the factors in a more general policy, which we shall have occasion to return to in considering problems of defense, the *force de frappe,* and nuclear strategy as a whole.

VII

MILITARY POLICY

The Two Goals of Military Policy

Defense and Diplomacy. There is in general a tendency to confuse two goals involved in military policy: defense and diplomacy. Of course, the two goals are always linked. Defense policy serves diplomacy, and diplomacy assures defense; but the distinction seems basic to me. For instance, Sweden and Switzerland have a military policy whose only goal is one of defense against a potential foreign enemy. Neither of them uses its military force or its power to obtain diplomatic advantages on the international scene. But the nature of weapons is such that today, there is discussion in both Sweden and Switzerland over whether defense does not necessitate, in the final analysis, the possession of nuclear weapons.

A classic, though perhaps inadequate distinction is that between great powers and small powers. A "great power" is a state that is capable of defending itself alone against any other state; in other words, one that has a chance of succeeding in a bilateral conflict with any other state. In this perspective, there are only two great powers in the world today: the Soviet Union and the United States. But does this mean that we can continue to divide the world into

the two categories of great powers and lesser powers? I do not believe so; for at the other end of the ladder, we already encounter
small states having no diplomatic leverage based on military
strength, and between these two extremes, a whole series of intermediary cases. In the past, at the time of individual and separate
nation-states, there was, on the one hand, the notion of individual
defense and, on the other hand, individual diplomatic intervention,
founded on military strength. Diplomatic intervention could take
place either in a limited sector at the borders, against a neighboring
state, or in the whole international field. Another distinction between the great power and a lesser power is that the diplomatic
objectives of great powers involve intervention in the whole international field and not only in border regions.

During the past thirty to fifty years, the idea of collective defense
and that of collective diplomatic intervention have developed
greatly. Hence today, in theory, the military policy of a state may be
concerned with collective defense, individual defense, limited individual diplomatic intervention, worldwide individual diplomatic
intervention, and collective worldwide diplomatic intervention.

All this seems terribly abstract, unless we translate it into concrete national examples. If we take Germany, for instance, we find
collective defense to the exclusion of any idea of individual defense,
and collective diplomatic intervention conceived only in the area
covered by the Atlantic Alliance. Neither individual defense, nor
individual diplomatic intervention based on military strength, nor
collective worldwide diplomatic intervention is provided for. In the
case of France, one aspect of military policy consists in attempting to
maintain at the same time: (1) individual defense, much more developed under the Fifth than under the Fourth Republic; (2) collective defense, in the limited area covered by the Atlantic Alliance;
(3) intervention based on individual strength, for the most part in
the ex-Empire, both in Africa and at one time, in Asia; (4) collective diplomatic intervention in the world — by the end of the
Fourth Republic, the wish had already been expressed that the Atlantic Alliance should work throughout the world and not only in

the limited geographic zone for which it had been defined in the 1949 treaty; (5) individual diplomatic intervention on a worldwide level, also based in part on military strength.

This link between the military and the diplomatic has always been one of General de Gaulle's major preoccupations, even before he became a general. I remind you of the situation from 1934 to 1938, and its relevance to the present. Why was the Maginot Line policy bad? Because it was bound to lead to Munich, for diplomacy was weak not only because of the diplomats, but because the diplomats had no military policy at their disposal. More precisely, at Munich, the most Daladier could have said to the Germans was: "If you attack us, we will defend ourselves"; but he could not say: "If you attack Czechoslovakia, we will attack you," because everyone knew full well that the French army was only trained to take the defensive, that the whole French military strategy was geared to respond to an attack against the Maginot Line. The absence of offensive weapons killed diplomacy.

The conclusion to be drawn, according to General de Gaulle, is that there is no diplomacy without offensive weapons, i.e., without the possibility of using for diplomatic purposes a military threat other than defense against attack. I believe that the *force de frappe* is largely a consequence of this reasoning. In this sense, Fifth Republic thinking on atomic weapons differs greatly from its equivalent under the Fourth. However, in the past (as I mentioned in the chapter on the Fourth Republic) there was an almost constant link between the notion of security and that of independence. In other words, the more independent its power, the more independent a state feels, and the more it will feel that its security is assured. Diplomatic strength and military strength go largely together.

Now, it happens that in Europe in 1964, and at least since 1949, the situation is the opposite. In other words, the more American forces there are on the continent, and the more the US finds itself directly engaged on the European continent, the greater Europe's security will be, and the less independent it will be. A reduction in the American presence, to the detriment of security, would be a step toward greater independence. The great difficulty is to find a compromise at a time when security and independence go hand in hand, but probably inversely.

Military Power and Political Role. For General de Gaulle, however, it is military strength in itself that must ensure both independence and security. He declared on January 31, 1962, "Never was it more true that the destiny of France is linked to its military power." The formula itself presents difficulties of translation. Suppose that a German Defense Minister made a speech tomorrow, maintaining: "Never was it more true that the destiny of Germany is linked to its military strength. . . ." I would like to see the reactions of the foreign press, and the French press in particular. . . . But we must examine the statement in itself. It is based on fact only very partially. A consideration of this point would appear indispensable.

What, indeed, were General de Gaulle's diplomatic successes in 1945? They were considerable: France was the fourth occupying power in Germany, and France was a permanent member of the Security Council. Yet, what was the military power of France at the time? . . . Practically nil. Material dependence on the United States? . . . Total. Despite that, there were spectacular diplomatic successes. Indo-China, Algeria: How did French military strength compare to the Viet-Minh or the FLN? . . . Overwhelming superiority. Political results: slight. Suez — and there is a point I have never understood concerning the *force de frappe* — Great Britain was a nuclear power; France was not. What was the difference in the treatment of the two countries by the United States? None. But one of the arguments put forth in favor of the *force de frappe* is that in order to receive consideration by the United States, one must be a nuclear power. Great Britain was a nuclear power in 1956; the advantage she derived was strictly nil.

The Position of Great Britain. The example of Great Britain is, however, extremely interesting for us in considering French military policy; for we might note that if we were in London today, we would employ practically the same terminology and the same ideas in speaking of British policy, whether we were speaking of strictly military considerations or of the political conclusions that derive from them.

In November, 1963, Patrick Gordon Walker, then Foreign Minister of the Labour Shadow Cabinet, declared: "We believe that the best solution for the Atlantic Alliance lies in an idea originally proposed by France. There should be a Directory to deal with broad policy covering nuclear weapons, European powers, etc." On February 26, 1966 during the House of Commons debate on defense policy, Defense Minister Thorneycroft stated: "The only defense we have against a threat of such attack is the ability to strike back, the knowledge that we can strike back at any enemy with an indestructible form of retaliation." And above all, he added (words that might have been used by de Gaulle or Pompidou): "Of course the world can change. . . . It may be that the Atlantic Alliance will grow, or that the conception of a more united Europe will develop. . . . If these political institutions grow, it may be possible to have some sharing even closer than we have been attempting. But to abandon the deterrent now, before the discussion has started, before the institutions have even begun the first flicker of growth, would be an extraordinary renunciation. It would not be an abdication of our defense, but of our rôle in the world." On the other hand, speaking for the opposition, Mr. Healey used the same language as the French leaders had used in 1960: "The contribution we make by maintaining the capacity for intervention outside Europe is of no less value to the west — indeed, in practical terms, is of more value — than troops who are on manoeuvres somewhere in the North German plain."[1] This statement could have come straight from Paris.

My purpose is to emphasize the community of problems regarding military policy that are shared by France and Great Britain, and which broadly account for the rivalry between the two countries.

[1] United Kingdom, *Parliamentary Debates, Fifth Series,* Vol. 690, House of Commons, 26 February 1964, pp. 458–475.

France and Nuclear Strategy

The Record at the End of the Fourth Republic. I refer you to a small brochure published by the UNR (Union pour la Nouvelle République — the political party formed in 1958 in support of de Gaulle — it has remained the majority party in the Assembly since then) entitled: *Pourquoi une force atomique française?*, which is well assembled and useful, whether one is for or against the different points it considers. One of the objections refuted in this brochure is the contention that the atomic force only serves the policy of power of General de Gaulle. The reply is: "If one accepted this objection, one would have to conclude that Félix Gaillard, Mendès-France, Edgar Faure, Guy Mollet, and Bourgès-Manoury are the most devoted partisans of the Fifth Republic. . . ." The paragraph concludes: "De Gaulle did not invent anything, he only accelerated an evolution that had become irreversible."

Indeed, the successive stages under the Fourth Republic show to what extent there was a steady evolution toward the construction of an atomic weapon. Under Mendès-France, in December, 1954, the Council of Ministers examined the question of the development of an atomic bomb, without making any decision. Under Edgar Faure came the development of the production of plutonium and the plans for the factory to separate isotopes, which was eventually built at Pierrelatte. Under Guy Mollet in 1956, there was a five-year plan for nuclear testing; and finally, the Gaillard Government decided on the construction of the atomic bomb which was tested at Reggane on February 13, 1960, and which was applauded by General de Gaulle: "Hurrah for France! Since this morning, she is stronger and more free!"

Why did the Fourth Republic undertake to build an atomic bomb? It was simply because there was, as I mentioned earlier, an astounding reversal in world strategy. Until the Russians possessed both atomic bombs *and* the possibility of delivering them across the ocean, the security of Europe was assured by American coverage, or by the American nuclear umbrella. Europeans felt secure because they were sure that the Russians were sure that the Americans would surely bomb Russia if the Russians attacked.

Then, the Soviet Union acquired the possibility of destroying the United States. Out of this fact grew the counter-reaction of fear on the part of the Europeans that an American President would no longer be willing to defend an objective lying outside the geographic limits of the United States. From that time on, the psychological situation was reversed. Whereas before 1955 the Europeans begged the United States never to use the atomic threat, to recall General MacArthur, to go slowly with nuclear armament, after 1955 they sought to press the United States to brandish the atomic threat because they feared that the United States would not do so in the defense of Europe. The idea of building an atomic force, not equal to that of the United States or the Soviet Union but at least capable of acting as a detonator, gradually won support. In writing the words that follow about General de Gaulle, Walter Lippmann should have realized that this form of French reasoning concerning nuclear weapons had already become military policy under the Fourth Republic:

> If France could make the first nuclear strike, one which compelled the United States to join her, the ultimate decision of nuclear war or peace is no longer in Washington. The *force de frappe* is a device to engage the United States, so that the initiative in nuclear strategy would be mainly in Continental Europe.[2]

This was exactly the intention behind the creation of a French atomic force in 1957–58: to acquire the possibility of constraining the United States to intervene, even though it did not wish to do so.

The Financial and Technical Debate. In order to acquire an atomic force, if others are unwilling to provide bombs and delivery systems, one must build one's own; and this raises the problem of the financial and technical debate over nuclear armament. I do not propose to enter here into the details covered in the innumerable publications concerning the *force de frappe.* I merely wish to

[2] Walter Lippmann, *Western Unity and the Common Market,* Boston, Little, Brown and Company, 1962, p. 8.

add, in all fairness, that the reply given by the "Cercle d'études de l'Armée Nouvelle" (an anonymous UNR group supporting the government's nuclear policy)[3] to the book published by the Club Jean Moulin (a group of intellectuals dedicated to public discussion of political, social, and economic issues),[4] is extremely interesting. At present, the debate is wide open.

There is open debate over the costs involved in the *force de frappe* because financial estimates vary to an extraordinary degree. In the first place, until now, all financial predictions have been proven false in practice. To cite one example: the installations at Pierrelatte were supposed to cost two billion francs — the present figures total five billion, and no one knows yet what the final figures will be. The cost of maintaining nuclear weapons is very high, and difficult to calculate for future years. No one knows exactly when a given form of defense provided for by the *loi-programme* will be outdated, and will necessitate the development of a new alternative.

In addition to the difficulty involved in arriving at a precise figure on cost, the quarrel over the percentage of such cost in the national budget remains open. The argument in favor of the atomic force holds that the percentage of the gross national product devoted to defense has constantly decreased since 1959. The level in the United States has been maintained around 10.5 per cent to 10.7 per cent from 1959–63; in Great Britain, around 7.5 per cent; while in France, the level has decreased from 7.9 per cent in 1959 to 6.9 per cent in 1963. Germany's level is 6 per cent, while Italy's is around 4 per cent of its gross national product (which no one would think of criticizing). Hence, one argument in favor of atomic weapons: the cost can be borne, since it is decreasing. The UNR brochure is very interesting because of its silence in this regard. It asserts, notably, that great economies have been made, without any mention of the Algerian war; no account is taken of the fact that certain military costs naturally decreased following the Évian agreements.

Also being discussed is the cost of the "second generation" after

[3] In the UNR monthly *Nouvelle Frontière*, January, 1964.
[4] *La Force de frappe et le citoyen*, Éditions du Seuil, 1963.

1970 — I refer you to other authors for the terminology — and the effect on French economic development of the total nuclear effort and expenditure. According to the UNR, the expenditure is highly productive: "Its multiplier effect will have repercussions on the levels of technology and industrial production. . . . If one thinks that in thirteen years, under the Fourth Republic, the State spent seventy billion NF for an army that could not resist for two days along the Rhine, one will appreciate . . . ," etc. This argument based on economic development is echoed even in those quarters most hostile to the Fifth Republic — for instance, a number of articles in *France-Observateur* (an opposition newspaper) run along such lines. On the other hand — surprise! — it was not a Leftist weekly, but the moderate and quiet *Figaro Littéraire* which, in a series of articles that appeared between January 30 and March 5, 1964, set about demonstrating, with supporting evidence, that the military nuclear effort was highly detrimental to scientific research and technological development.

I humbly confess that I am unable to reach a conclusion out of all these disparate factors, for the evaluations are so different, and the arguments involved so opposed and so seductive on all sides, that I can hardly see how one can say what is detrimental or favorable to technical development. On the other hand, what strikes me personally, and makes me strongly skeptical and hostile in regard to the *force de frappe,* is the wide gap in relation to the major nuclear powers. In this respect, the argument contained in the UNR brochure, maintaining that France is ahead of the United States and the Soviet Union with the *Mystère* and the future submarines, leaves me, to say the least, with great reservations. When I see that the budget for the French nuclear force is approximately equal to the research budget of the United States or the Soviet Union, I am drawn to the conclusion — perhaps wrongly, since I am not a technician — that with such a large research budget, the two major powers should be able to maintain their advance permanently, if not to increase it. To which one might reply that there is no point in continuing expansion at the stage they have arrived at, given the possibility of mutual destruction . . . etc. I am little impressed by this argument, and as I shall indicate later, I am likewise little impressed by a similar form of strategic reasoning. In the meantime, the financial and technical debate was considered ended by the majority vote of the Assembly, and today French defense policy is organized in such a manner as to take account of the decision that was reached.

Defense Organization. I believe that the organization of French defense policy was expounded most clearly in an article by Defense Minister Pierre Messmer.[5] French military policy at present is based on three elements: the strategic force, i.e., the *force de frappe;* the intervention force or *force d'intervention;* and, according to the currently fashionable abbreviation, the DOT, or the *Défense opérationnelle du Territoire* (Operational defense of the Territory).

The *force d'intervention* and the DOT are being progressively sacrificed to the *force de frappe* in the budget. In other words, in expenditure and investment, the three forces basically exist on paper. But the strategic force receives the financial allocations.

The *force de frappe* depends directly on the authority of the President of the Republic, according to Article 5 of the decree, which stated: "The Command of the strategic air force is entrusted with the carrying into operation of this force, upon the order of engagement given by the President of the Republic, President of the Defense Council, Head of the Army. . . ."[6] It is worth pointing out in passing that this decree largely dispossessed the Prime Minister of the military powers that he held theretofore by virtue of the organization provided for in 1962. What is extremely striking in Messmer's article is that NATO has completely disappeared. The strategic force is conceived as independent, the *force d'intervention* as national, in order to be capable of intervening wherever French presence is maintained throughout the world. As for the defense of French territory, this is even more national. It is difficult to see how the collective concern for Atlantic defense enters into such a military policy.

Since 1958, a number of concrete steps have been taken, whether prompted by ill humor or more deliberate: withdrawal of the Medi-

[5] *Revue de Défense Nationale,* May, 1963.
[6] *Journal Officiel,* January 19, 1964.

terranean fleet from Atlantic command in case of war; maintaining few divisions in Germany (the divisions returning from Algeria did not resume their normal positions), refusal to grant new bases to the United States or to allow the building of missile bases, unlike other countries.

The maneuvers in the Jura region in 1963 did not particularly please the Germans, since they provided for a purely national defense and the preliminary destruction of German cities. The German military observers were subsequently informed that these maneuvers had taken place in order to demonstrate that solidarity was indispensable.

"National" Defense. The rejection of the Moscow Treaty of July 25, 1963 on the banning of nuclear testing in the atmosphere, in outer space, and under the sea (a limited list excluding the banning of underground tests), must be understood within the context of a nuclear-based national defense.

A comment is called for here. I do not believe that any French Head of State or Head of Government would have agreed to signing this treaty, for it would have meant that overnight France would be the only country to end its military policy completely, and to change it from top to bottom. I believe that, given the stage of progress, the commitment of credits, and the construction of nuclear weapons, it was virtually impossible to sign the Moscow Treaty. This said, General de Gaulle rejected it in much more precise and political words, declaring in Lyon on September 29, 1963:

> It is with the same intention of ensuring that others should not become masters of our destiny that we, too, are in the process of endowing ourselves with nuclear weapons. For it is a fact of gigantic proportions and without precedent that, at the present time, the very life of every nation is literally at the mercy of whoever possesses such weapons, unless in some quarter the same means exist, and the wicked know that they will be struck peremptorily, should they venture to commit aggression.

And further:

> For us, the question is thus to decide whether we, too, should dispose of such arms of dissuasion ... or whether we should trans-

mit to the Anglo-Saxons all our chances of life and death, and certain of our economic possibilities of tomorrow. That question has been settled; we have decided — without in any way renouncing our attachment to our allies across the Atlantic — to acquire what is necessary to defend ourselves, and to assure us of the knowledge and realizations which, without any doubt, will command the future.

And he added: "France would freely renounce [her weapons] if the day were to come when all those who possessed such arms were to disarm, rather than forbidding such arms to those who do not possess them." The general theme is: "France will not accept that two privileged states should be the sole possessors of nuclear strength." This is hardly complimentary to Great Britain, since she is considered incorporated, somehow or other, with the United States. We shall return later to the political aspects of this statement.

I should like to dwell for a moment on its military aspects. The argument that it is not possible to threaten the Russians with a small force is not immediately convincing. The destruction of atomic submarines is impossible in the present state of technology; they are unreachable. "The smaller you are, the more secure you are," General Gallois explains. The reasoning is simple and so seductive that its absurdity is not immediately apparent: the state that would be best protected by the possession of an atomic bomb, with a plane capable of delivering it, would therefore be Monaco, or Luxemburg. This is very easy to comprehend: the stake that Luxemburg would represent for a future aggressor is not worth the risk that even one atomic bomb, even of the size of that dropped on Hiroshima, would pose; thus, he would not attack, since the risk is greater than the value of the stake. It seems to me that in this whole line of reasoning there is one major flaw — a psychological one. Personally, I do not believe that any French government, even that of General de Gaulle, could enter the atomic poker game individually — convincing the Soviet Union, for instance, that France would risk suicide over a diplomatic account with a country whose forces of destruction are infinitely more powerful than her own. Whatever limits one sets on the intervention of public opinion in matters of military policy or even diplomacy, it seems to me that there is an insuperable threshold in the credibility of the resort to the atomic threat.

An Explanation of the Cuban Crisis. But above all, it appears that there exists in French military reasoning today a profound lack of understanding of current American strategy. The United States is largely responsible for this state of affairs, in that changes in strategy are made without ever really consulting NATO partners. It is interesting to consider the opposite conclusions that were drawn in Washington and Paris from the Cuban crisis of October, 1962. In the eyes of many Frenchmen, strategists included, it was the atomic poker game that allowed Kennedy to force Khrushchev to retreat, and it was American nuclear power that won the showdown. Now, the whole strategy of McNamara, currently implemented by NATO, is founded on the opposite reasoning: it was American conventional forces that won the diplomatic victory.

What happened in Cuba? . . . Upon discovering the Soviet launching pads, Kennedy said to Khrushchev: "Remove them or my navy and air force will destroy your bases." Since there were no Soviet navy and air force in the area, the only possible counter-threat open to Khrushchev in response to the American threat was the nuclear threat. But in order for the nuclear threat to function, it must be credible. Now, it was *not* credible that Khrushchev would risk the suicide of the Soviet Union for an objective as far off as Cuba. Since this was not credible, it could not be used; thus, a nuclear counter-threat was to no avail and the superiority of a local American conventional force (air force, navy) won the diplomatic victory. The lesson that the Americans drew concerning Europe was that if there were not a formidable effort to build up conventional forces on the European continent, we would risk finding ourselves in Berlin in the Cuban-situation-in-reverse, where, this time, the Western nuclear counter-threat would rightly be non-credible, when faced with a conventional threat on the part of the Soviet Union. In order to arrive at the level of credible nuclear threat and counter-threat, there must be a possibility of a minimum of conventional counter-threat, in response to a Soviet threat, in order to raise the stakes.

It was precisely for this reason that the United States begged the Europeans to understand the necessity for increasing conventional forces to ensure European security. But the Europeans replied by playing deaf: the French because they wanted their *force de frappe,* the Italians because they wanted neither. The Germans are more or less alone in fulfilling their commitments. General de Gaulle pretends to believe that the United States might abandon Europe, but since his policies wind up irritating the Americans, we run into statements like Senator Fulbright's threat: "If you don't behave, we will withdraw." This is a perfectly vain threat, for the Americans will not withdraw, but since Fulbright made the statement, it lends strength to General de Gaulle's argument, when he feigns belief that withdrawal is possible.

The Insoluble Problem

In reality, the basic problem is unfortunately insoluble. It has not changed since 1949. The atomic poker game necessitates, for both military and diplomatic reasons, the concentration of decision-making power in the hands of one person. It is not possible for the poker hand to be played by a commission, by a meeting of Heads of Government, or anything of the kind. It is inevitable that the person involved should be the President of the United States. This is one side of the fence. On the other side lies the fact that no thoughtful European statesman could tolerate the fact that the physical fate of his fellow citizens should be left indefinitely in the hands of a friendly, but far-off Head of State. In the case of General de Gaulle, there is the additional example of the Strasbourg episode — the first-hand experience that there is a strong chance that all members of a coalition will not evaluate the dangers to be faced in the same manner, and that it is perfectly likely and possible that, one day, the leader of the coalition will not deem vital the defense of a point considered as such by the member of the Alliance most directly involved.

Consequently, on the one hand, a monopoly of decision-making power is inevitable in order to ensure security and to play the atomic poker game; but on the other hand, this situation is perfectly intolerable. It is for this reason that there is no good alternative to the *force de frappe,* which I personally consider to be a bad policy.

If we take, for instance, the reply of the Club Jean Moulin (which, to my knowledge, was drawn up by the "Europeans," and especially by Étienne Hirsch, former President of Euratom) we find the following: "French foreign policy ought to have as its primary objective, not national independence coupled with ambitions of European hegemony that lie above her means, but the building, stage by stage, of a multinational Europe that respects the personality of the member-states, while providing necessary cohesion to their community institutions." The idea is for a European *force de frappe.* But this raises two questions.

The first: What does a European *force de frappe* mean, without nuclear weapons in the hands of Germany? At this point, the last stake left to the West in negotiating with the East, as a counter-concession to a Soviet concession — the continued nuclear disarmament of Germany — would disappear. Furthermore, and above all, from the point of view of Atlantic policy and from the point of view of American policy, a European *force de frappe* would simply transpose to the level of Europe the problem of the French national *force de frappe,* but without resolving the problem in any way.

Either this European force would be a decoy — as are all the proposed "multilateral" or "multinational" forces — leaving the final decision in the hands of the President of the United States; or else it would create a second center of decision-making power. At that point, it would be no more acceptable to the United States than the French national *force de frappe.* The other proposed substitute solutions — for instance, a coordination of policies — do nothing but veil the supremacy of the American power of decision. I shall return to this point presently.

VIII

THE ATLANTIC ALLIANCE, THE USSR, AND CHINA

The Global Outlook of General de Gaulle

Rather than a concrete situation, my point of departure in this chapter will be what might be called the global outlook of General de Gaulle; for it is not possible to explain his Atlantic or European policies, and especially his relations with the Soviet Union and China, without taking into account this global outlook, which has the great quality of being perfectly clear, and of having been explained quite plainly on several occasions.

It seems to me that the most articulate text, and one which ought to have cleared up hosts of former misunderstandings, is the address delivered before the Congress of the United States in Washington, on April 25, 1960. I quote two excerpts: "But if, in material terms, the balance between the two camps which divide the universe may seem equal, morally, it is not. France made her choice. She has chosen to be on the side of the free peoples; she has chosen to be there with you." And further on: "I will even add that Federal Germany is rendering the greatest possible service to coexistence by incorporating itself as it does into Western Europe. Through the organization of a Western European ensemble, facing the bloc built by the Soviets, it will be possible to establish from the Atlantic to the Urals some equilibrium between these two zones which are comparable both in populations and in resources. Alone, such a balance may perhaps one day enable the old continent to bring a reconciliation between its two parts, to find peace within itself, to give a fresh start to its civilization and lastly to have the possibility, together with America, to help, in an atmosphere of serenity, the development of the unfavored masses of Asia and the awakening populations of Africa."[1]

I consider this text sufficiently clear because it brings out the central idea very plainly. In appearance, there is a contradiction. We encounter this contradiction again, moreover, in the press conference on January 31, 1964, where, in reply to a question on Latin America, General de Gaulle declared: "Of course the rivalry of the totalitarian camp and that of liberty, as well as the national ambitions which are at work under the cloak of ideologies do not fail to cause . . . ferments of all sorts."[2] There would appear to be a contradiction between, on the one hand, the opposition of ideologies and regimes (freedom, totalitarianism); and on the other hand, national ambitions (which are the reality) and ideologies (which are straw men, false appearances). I believe that the idea is relatively simple. It so happens that in the present situation there are free and totalitarian countries. So long as things remain this way, there will be a Western world, and there will be an Atlantic Alliance — what we must hope is that it will be strong enough to oppose the expansion of totalitarianism. But since regimes and ideologies are transitory, and nation-states are permanent, it may one day happen that totalitarianism will fade out in Europe, and then Europe will be able to re-create its unity — it being well understood that European unity means all of Europe west of the Urals.

[1] U.S. Government, 86th Congress, 2nd sess., *Congressional Record,* Vol. 106, Part 7, p. 8644.

[2] French Embassy: Press and Information Division, *Major Addresses, Statements and Press Conferences of General Charles de Gaulle* (May 19, 1958–January 31, 1964), 250.

Speaking of China at his press conference on January 31, General de Gaulle stated: "Within the Communist Church . . . appears the inevitable difference in national policies."[3] This is more than a statement of fact, it is the expression of a wish and of a conception of History. In the short run, there is a threat to freedom; but in the long run, this situation will come to an end, and this will be a happy day for France since the return to strictly national preoccupations will free her of American tutelage.

In his message to Parliament on December 11, 1962, General de Gaulle spoke of "The Atlantic Alliance *currently* necessary to the defense of the free world." At his press conference on January 31, he spoke of "The regime that currently dominates China." The two adverbs go together. It is because there is a totalitarian communism in China or in the Soviet Union that the Atlantic Alliance is necessary. But the hope is in the process of change: "When will the liberalization of the communist world permit a normalization in world politics?" It is here that we see immediately the principal difference between what we shall call, for the moment, the Gaullist outlook on the international scene (and I will demonstrate in a moment that it is largely shared by the French opposition to de Gaulle) and the American or German outlook.

In General de Gaulle's view, it is true that the East-West conflict exists, but it will not be eternal, and nothing must be done that would prevent a change on the world chessboard in case of a détente in the East-West conflict. In the American view, and even more in the German view, the East-West conflict will constitute the major axis of world politics for a long time to come: to worry about what will happen afterward is in the realm of prophecy and not politics. And, above all, to weaken the cohesion of the Western world, in the short run, for a problematic vision of the long run where the notion of a Western world would no longer hold meaning, is to do a disservice to the Western world. It is necessary to comprehend this divergence in order to understand why General de Gaulle opposes the Atlantic Community. Once again — and a crucial point

[3] *Ibid.,* pp. 256–257.

— we must distinguish between "Atlantic *Community*" and "Atlantic *Alliance*."

To allow an Atlantic Community to be created is to prevent the desired evolution; it is to "de-Europeanize" the Western half of Europe and to render impossible in advance the reunification of Europe with its liberalized Eastern regions. On January 14, 1963, at the famous press conference at which he rejected British membership in the Common Market, de Gaulle explained himself very plainly:

> Following Britain, other States . . . would or will want to enter the Common Market. . . . We would then have to envisage the construction of another Common Market. But the 11-member, then 13-member, and then perhaps 18-member Common Market that would be built would, without any doubt, hardly resemble the one the Six have built. Moreover, this Community growing in that way would be confronted with all the problems of its economic relations with a crowd of other States, and first of all with the United States. It is foreseeable that the cohesion of its members, who would be very numerous and very diverse, would not hold for long and that in the end there would appear a colossal Atlantic Community, under American dependence and leadership which would soon completely swallow up the European Community.

The Atlantic Community would destroy the vision of Western Europe today, and of a reunited Europe of tomorrow.

Where General de Gaulle went wrong, as I mentioned earlier in connection with Germany, was in thinking that Great Britain was hostile to this idea, while Germany might favor it. The opposite has proved to be the case: the Federal Republic represents the United States' real Trojan Horse. Indeed, for Germany, objective number one — the defense of Berlin — is a community objective. Liberal and anticommunist ideology inspires German policy much more than the notion of community. Thus, for Germany as for the United States, the Atlantic community is more important than the European community, and all notions of a Europe extending to the Urals is excluded. Italy subscribes to approximately the same notion,

because, for both Italy and Germany, the concern over equality
within the Alliance and the problem of a noncommunal Atlantic
Community do not arise in the same form as for France.

Equality and Consultation

As early as September 24, 1958, Paris sent a diplomatic note to
Washington requesting equality within the Alliance — proposing a
three-way Directory. What sort of equality would this be? Equality
à la George Orwell: some must be more equal than others. French
policy sought to see to it that France was included among those
more equal than the others. There were unofficial rumors to the effect that the Quai d'Orsay had communicated part of the note to
Rome, Bonn, The Hague, and Brussels — the part dealing with
equality *per se* — and that London had quickly communicated to
the same capitals the second part of the note dealing with the *égalité
à trois,* or the tripartite Directory.

It is a fact that there is a basic problem of equality within the
Atlantic Alliance. This issue is viewed a bit facilely by the Americans, on the one hand, and by the Germans and Italians on the
other. Part of the problem for the Americans is that it is very difficult to find either American diplomats or newspapers that have
truly appreciated the unequal character of the Atlantic Alliance —
I shall return to this point in the Conclusion. For the Germans
and the Italians, when compared to their situation in 1945, the
present situation is splendid already. We encounter somewhat the
same phenomenon in relation to European unity. It was far easier
for the Germans to renounce what they had not yet recovered than
it was for the French to abandon what they had. For Germany, the
situation is incomparably better than the total subjection to which
they were reduced by the victors in 1945. It is for this reason that the
Italians and Germans are much less sensitive than the English to
General de Gaulle's demand for equality within the Alliance.

How Can Equality Be Established? General de Gaulle is very
strongly hostile to supranationality, and even the prospect of majority decision within the Atlantic Alliance enters hardly at all into

his thinking. What he desires is, on the one hand, consultation, and on the other hand, the shaping of decisions by the ally most directly concerned. Consultation: when General de Gaulle recognized Communist China, the Germans had a legitimate right to complain, for it was contrary to the treaty of January 22, 1963. The United States could hardly complain, for General de Gaulle could always reply: When, indeed, have *you* consulted us?

Is Consultation Possible? The first reason why the United States could not and did not wish to consult goes back to the time of the Algerian War. At no point could the United States accept the idea of appearing in the United Nations as part of an alliance including the Netherlands, Belgium, Portugal, France, and Great Britain; i.e., all the colonial powers. This would have been an initial reason for avoiding Atlantic consultation on problems outside the geographic limits of the Alliance. But there is another factor inherent in the American system. The decision-making process within the American political system is so unwieldy and complicated that consultation with allies is, to say the least, difficult. Indeed, if consultation were to take place *before* the decision-making process, no choice would have been made and it would be hard to know what to consult on. But if there were consultation *after* a decision had been made, the decision-making process might have to be faced a second time. The upshot is that there is no consultation; partners are informed of decisions that have already been made. Every week in Paris, the ambassadors who make up the Council of Deputies meet in the NATO building at Porte Dauphine. In theory, they constitute the permanent element of consultation. In practice, either there is no consultation, or there is consultation on secondary issues. But as soon as a matter of any importance arises, a decision is made by Washington, which is kind enough to *inform* its partners. General de Gaulle proceeds in the same fashion in order to constrain the Americans to change their attitude. It is not certain that he will succeed.

The other issue is the *principle of the ally most directly concerned*. Here, it is proper to bring in General de Gaulle's attitude during the Cuban crisis of 1962. When Dean Acheson came to see the General at the time of the Cuban crisis, it seems that he was surprised by de Gaulle's faithfulness and firmness. At that point, Rome, Bonn, and London were rather reticent, and pleaded with the Americans to go slowly, not to play the nuclear poker game too far; while General de Gaulle, on the contrary, assured the United States of his unconditional support and recommended that it play the nuclear poker game all the way. Why? The first explanation is that in time of danger, ranks are closed, and complaints disappear temporarily. The second reason was not to give in to threat, to remain firm.

But the real reason, and the most important, in my view, is that the Cuban affair represented the hoped-for precedent — the opportunity to tell the United States: It is up to you to decide, and we will give you full support because Cuba is close to the United States. Only, if a similar crisis should occur in Europe, it is up to us to decide, and to you to support us unconditionally, in conformity with the theory of Alliance maintaining that each state has the right to decide for the collectivity in matters vital to its interests. This also formed the substance of the de Gaulle-Adenauer entente: it was up to the Germans to say what the Alliance should do concerning Berlin; it was up to the French to tell the Alliance what its Algerian policy and its North African policy in general should be. In this manner, the idea of equality in decision making is reconciled with the absence of mechanisms for vote by majority. I do not believe that allies like Germany or Italy can be expected to adopt this rule of the game. General de Gaulle's reply, as I have already indicated elsewhere, is that France will play the role of Europe until such time as the others are ready to join him.

I am convinced that one of the major tactical goals of General de Gaulle's foreign policy is to constrain the Americans to accept consultation. His technique is to attempt to build a Europe sharing his attitude, and to pursue unilateral policies toward Vietnam, Southeast Asia, and Latin America — not so much out of anti-Americanism, but so that the Americans will one day say: "Consult us first"; which would permit the reply: "On condition of reciprocity." I am convinced that the fundamental goal of de Gaulle's foreign policy since 1958 has been to achieve equality within the Alliance, while awaiting the day when the world will no longer be divided into two blocs.

The Enemy and the Enemy's Enemy

The Atlantic Alliance, in theory, is directed defensively against another bloc, and this is what leads us to consider policy toward the Soviet Union and China. The first aspect, in regard to policy toward the USSR, is de Gaulle's *hard line*. With the exception of 1960, General de Gaulle has been resolutely hostile to summit conferences. Why was 1960 an exception? It seems to me that at that time, de Gaulle had two reasons for accepting a summit conference: the first was that it would take place in Paris and that he would preside; the second was that everyone knew in advance that it would accomplish nothing. When Khrushchev realized that it would have no concrete results, moreover, he brought it to an abrupt ending over the U-2 incident.

Thus, in principle, General de Gaulle is opposed to summit conferences. It is noteworthy that this attitude is fundamentally different from that of all the Fourth Republic leaders. For instance, in the spring of 1955, when Premier Edgar Faure addressed the Senate concerning the ratification of the Paris Agreements, he declared: "If you do not ratify, the Americans will surely not come to a summit conference; if you do ratify, the Americans will surely come and the Russians, perhaps." This was the case in 1955. Why did the leaders of the Fourth Republic adopt this position? As I indicated elsewhere, when there was a summit conference, when the Big Four met, France was one of the Four Major Powers. And that was about the only time. Why did General de Gaulle refuse? Because the Big Four are Four only when the issue concerned is Germany. (This is the sole reason for being four. If the issues concern the major world powers, India or Japan should be included; if the major UN powers are involved, there are five and not four.)

Now, in regard to Germany, there are three basic issues: the

Oder-Neisse line, Berlin, and the status of East Germany. On these three questions, there can only be two possible outcomes at a summit conference: a total absence of results or unilateral concessions by the West; for any change in the status quo is a Western concession. What purpose is served by holding a summit conference if it is only to make unilateral concessions without reciprocity? Consequently, the Fifth Republic took a much harder and more intransigent line in policy toward the Soviet Union than the Governments of the Fourth Republic. We encounter the same attitude regarding the Oder-Neisse line: the line may well be definitive, but this is still more of a reason not to participate in a summit conference, for what purpose would be served by accepting it officially, if it were not in exchange for a counter-concession? Since there are no counter-concessions, it is useless to stage a meeting in order to acknowledge this fact together, for that would only constitute a defeat for the West.

The second aspect of policy toward the USSR: *cordiality*. To begin with, because this produces immediate benefits on the domestic political scene. The content of the communist daily, *L'Humanité,* in regard to General de Gaulle is always rather heartening in periods of cordiality between Paris and Moscow. But there are other considerations.

Except in periods of tension, General de Gaulle prefers to use the word "Russia" in speaking of the Soviet Union. This reflects once again the abiding belief in nations which endure longer than passing ideologies. The ideal of a broad union from the Atlantic to the Urals is contained in General de Gaulle's speech welcoming Khrushchev, during the latter's visit to Paris in June, 1960, where he spoke of "France and Russia, daughters of the same Europe." This means — as I mentioned earlier in connection with Germany (and a fact which is often incomprehensible for Germans or Americans) — that Karl Marx or Stalin, as well as Dante and the concentration camps, for better or for worse, belong to the same culture, the same European civilization; and that there does not exist a so-called "West" ending at the demarcation line between Eastern and Western Europe, with a region of barbarians lying to the other side of that line.

Thus, Russia is not bad in herself: it is possible to have good relations with her because she belongs to the same Western civilization as we do. In 1959 de Gaulle advanced his version of the two camps in the world today. They are not at all the two one might expect: they are the "haves" and the "have-nots." Russia more and more belongs to the "haves," to the bourgeois nations; and China assumes the leadership of the "have-nots." This is yet another reason for not adopting a uniformly intransigent position toward the Soviet Union, since the evolution of the world is bringing her progressively into the camp of the Western industrial nations.

There was a time when General de Gaulle spoke of what he called "the yellow peril," which caused much ink to be spilled because of its racist implications. Today, the situation has changed somewhat. More recently, it was Khrushchev who spoke of the yellow peril, or more precisely, of the racism of Mao Tse-tung, who groups the yellow and black races on one side, and the whites on the other. But, if there is indeed a rapprochement between the Soviet Union and the West, and if cordial relations can be maintained alongside diplomatic intransigence, why did de Gaulle recognize Communist China?

Here, I shall sum up the situation in a simple paradox: *The United States has become Gaullist, and General de Gaulle has ceased to be a Gaullist because he is not American.* This requires some explanation. The United States has become Gaullist. We learned in school that "the enemy of my enemy is my friend." But what is United States policy today? "The enemy of my enemy is even more my enemy than my first enemy." The devil is in Moscow; Moscow is having difficulties with China; to whose rescue shall I fly? To the rescue of Moscow. Why? Because American foreign policy has at least two goals: the first is anticommunism; the second is the defense of peace.

American leaders consider that the Soviet leaders are reasonable men, that they are men who sincerely desire peace and with whom one can talk, with whom one can conclude implicit "gentlemen's agreements." They are no longer considered the apostles of violence (as any good communist should be if the communists were the way Americans imagine them to be). They have become instead something like a French-style communist, that is, having revolutionary ideas, but at heart as little of a revolutionary as a second-generation socialist.

The vision of the Soviet Union has thus been appreciably modified in the United States and has begun to resemble what General de Gaulle was talking about in 1959: China is the leader of the world revolution, whereas Russia is a fairly satisfied state above all concerned with its internal economic development. But then, why does de Gaulle oppose American policy? why did he refuse to sign the Moscow Treaty? why did he recognize Communist China? In the first place, because the Moscow Treaty marked a return to Yalta — to the domination of the world by the Big Two. Aside from the reasons given earlier, in connection with the nuclear program being too far advanced to abandon, the Moscow Treaty was likewise unacceptable because it would ensure the domination of the Big Two over the rest of the world, and thereby mark a return to the spirit of Yalta.

General de Gaulle would go so far as to accept the dissemination of nuclear weapons. Personally, I cannot believe that he would endorse General Gallois' theory that the maximum dissemination of nuclear weapons is the best guarantee of peace — this would mean that true peace would not be achieved until the day when each of the earth's three billion men would carry a miniature bomb around in his pocket. I believe that General de Gaulle is perfectly conscious of the monstrous diplomatic danger involved in the dissemination of nuclear weapons, but he considers that the Soviet-American duopoly is even more dangerous, insofar as it stands for world domination by the Big Two and prevents the interplay of nation-states.

One of the reasons for recognizing Communist China would thus be to bar the way to the domination of the Big Two and, if possible, to break up one bloc, while awaiting the day when the other bloc will break up in turn.

The Recognition of Communist China

An incidental remark: the recognition of Communist China put de Gaulle's Leftist opposition in an extremely embarrassing position, since he had in fact done what they had demanded for many years. On the diplomatic level, the first consequences of the recognition were negative, since Formosa severed diplomatic relations with France. One of the avowed goals of the recognition was to demonstrate that it was possible to have relations with both Chinas — which indeed would have rescued the United States from its own difficult position. The advantages of recognition are not so much of an economic character. Trade can indeed develop without diplomatic recognition. The first motive was *prestige*. In discussing the problem, everyone acknowledged that France's position within the Atlantic Alliance resembled that of China in the Eastern world — although, no matter how important France is, its real strength does not appear to me completely equal to that of China, to say the least. But look at the commentaries throughout the world: on the one hand, Russia and the United States; on the other, France and China. It is most flattering!

Discussion with the United States is difficult, to begin with because certain arguments basic to the US position are unacceptable in France. In a fairly amusing editorial there is a passage that appears very true to me:

> Certain Americans recall that they lost 30,000 boys in Korea, and that they have not forgotten that fact, but melancholy is not policy. If it were, France would no longer have the slightest relationship with Algeria, and this would redound to the great misfortune of the West.[4]

I believe that this is indeed an issue over which Franco-American debate is impossible, for the entire American press asserts more or less explicitly: We cannot recognize the country that killed our soldiers in Korea. Now whether applied to Franco-German rela-

[4] "Why All the Commotion," *La Nation*, January 20, 1964.

tions or Franco-Algerian relations, this argument meets little sympathy in France, because France has indeed gone far in relations
with her ex-enemies. But another point brought out by *La Nation*
also merits some comment:

> The principal Atlantic power seems indeed to conceive of its
> relations with other powers in the same manner as the Sun King
> conceived of his with his courtesans. This conception is outdated,
> in the first place, because there are no longer any courtesans . . .

Applied solely to the international situation, this means that equality with the United States must be re-established. "We do indeed
have the right to recognize Communist China if we decide to." The
US Government replies, justifiedly in my view: "You can do
whatever you wish, but who bears the consequences? If your
Asian policy takes a bad turn, who ends up paying financially, economically, militarily? Not you, but us. Consequently, you are
assuming no risks in taking unilateral initiatives."

The French Government would then continue: "So then you
admit that it is because you are the strongest that you should decide everything within the Atlantic Alliance. Then, let us make
our nuclear weapons in order to end this dependence due to your
strength. If you have the right to make all the decisions because
you must bear the economic and military consequences, then the
Alliance is based on power, which you constantly deny." The dialogue could go on indefinitely, but of course it poses this question:
Is there in the policy of General de Gaulle an element of *permanent
hostility to the United States?*

Mr. Couve de Murville said one day that it would be "completely
ridiculous" to imagine that there was the slightest element of anti-
Americanism in French policy. We shall therefore take the risk of
being ridiculous in believing that in all of General de Gaulle's attitudes, there is an excessive element of personal memories. The relations between the Free French and Roosevelt from 1940 to 1944
have not ceased to influence Franco-American relations. In addition, there is an anti-American feeling in France, which we shall
attempt to analyze later.

But the United States is not alone in declaring that the recognition of Communist China poses a very grave problem. There are likewise France's other allies. We must therefore examine briefly the *diplomatic theory underlying the recognition.* One idea is that expounded by former Premier Edgar Faure in an interview with the *Figaro* on January 9, 1964 — an interview that is all the more important in that, allegedly, Faure made up both the questions and the answers, and submitted the entire text to the Élysée before publication.

Mr. Faure explained: "The tensions that once existed between France and China because of the colonial problem and the Algerian War no longer exist." Here, we encounter the bilateral conception of international affairs already expressed by General de Gaulle in his conversations with Stalin in December, 1944. Since there is no direct national opposition between France and the USSR, we can conclude a treaty.

But there is more: there is an implicit theory espoused not only by France, but by the International Olympics Committee as well. Recognition should not imply any moral criteria; once a government is master of a territory, it should be recognized. This was the policy of the International Olympics Committee, whose president is an American, and which recognizes Communist China. Nationalist China only represents Formosa. This is a fine and acceptable theory. Only, France is a close ally of the Federal Republic of Germany. In Germany, concern immediately arose over the idea that such a theory could be applied to East Germany. How could the French reply? To begin with (and this is what seems to have been done) by sending all the accredited French ambassadors throughout the world to explain to the governments to which they were accredited, that there was no relation between East Germany and Communist China. Why? Because the German Democratic Republic has a less liberal regime? Because the Federal Republic is the sole legitimate government and the other is not? This is the argument that is generally advanced.

Since May, 1964, a third theory has been put forth by France, which is reasonably close to the German theory on the two Germanies: the regime in East Germany is a foreign government. In his latest declarations, Mr. Couve de Murville maintained that the East German regime is a disguised Soviet government. There is no reason to recognize a regime that does not exist, since it is, in fact, a non-German regime.

The recognition of China is thus not a purely bilateral affair concerning only China and France, but a problem confronting a number of states: that of the application of the French theory of recognition. This theory has not ceased to have repercussions in European politics in general, and in Franco-German politics in particular.

"A Worldwide Policy"

So far we have examined de Gaulle's attitude toward the Atlantic world, and toward the Soviet Union and China. We must return, in conclusion, to the formula employed at the press conference of January 31, 1964, which bears the imprint of General de Gaulle's style: "France, because she is France, must pursue a worldwide policy." At first sight, of course, this would appear to be a series of truisms. But upon closer inspection, it is a whole theory: "France, because she is France" — this means that others are not in the same position; this means that independent of the situation of power and strength, France has rights and duties that are entirely different from those of other countries. Moreover, the pursuit of a worldwide policy is a mission that is not within the reach of all states. If we took an inventory of the states whose leaders claim that they must "pursue a worldwide policy," we would finish very quickly — unless we were to consider worldwide commerce to be the equivalent of a worldwide policy. What are the means open to France in pursuit of this worldwide policy that she has a claim to "because she is France"? Is such a policy possible? What does it mean concretely, when compared with what the French people desire?

One last comment: whatever be the means, the psychological reality also has its importance. In other words, in the absence of means, one can pass off for a force what is simply a word, a presence.

Try for a moment to pretend that you are General de Gaulle: put yourself in his place. The United States repeats endlessly that the influence that you can achieve through your power is insignificant; and yet, when you have your Minister of Information read the final sentence of a communiqué dealing with Vietnam, following a meeting of the Council of Ministers, the President of the United States issues a statement, and the world press flashes five-column headlines. Would *you* really be convinced that your deeds and gestures were of no importance?

IX

EVALUATION AND CONCLUSION

The Content of Policy

The Theory of Variations. Let us consider first what I have called the "theory of *variations*." The foreign policy of the Fifth Republic has changed often; it looks like a sinusoidal curve, with veritable about-faces. The Soviet Union appears at times as a friend (Khrushchev's visit to Paris in 1960, Edgar Faure's trip to the Soviet Union in 1964), and at other times as an archenemy. China was the "yellow peril" in 1959; in 1964 diplomatic relations were established. The UN was looked upon with scorn for many years; but U Thant was welcomed cordially to Paris in 1964. Toward the United States — unfailing ally in times of crisis, but almost constant criticisms and policies designed to provoke annoyance. Africa: at times a center of interest; at other times, viewed with indifference. On balance, even a Government diplomatic adviser could state publicly: "In truth, we have had several successive policies since 1958."

The Theory of Continuity in Policy. Parallel to these *variations*, there is the question of continuity in policy versus change. Does the foreign policy of the Fifth Republic continue or break with the basic policy decisions of the Fourth Republic? In my view, there is a very noticeable continuity in relation to 1958. The major decisions of the Fourth Republic have been maintained. It remains to be seen whether there was any choice, whether the choice was deliberate, or whether it was made of necessity. *"L'Europe des Six,"* with a Franco-German foundation, was a decision made under the Fourth Republic, which the future leaders of the Fifth Republic had fought against wholeheartedly before 1958. Decolonization was expanded to a point that Fourth Republic leaders would hardly have dared to envisage. Fidelity to the Atlantic Alliance, to a Western camp of freedom facing the totalitarian world, was a decision dating back to 1947 and confirmed by the Atlantic Alliance in 1949. The Fifth Republic did not depart from that course.

The Objectives. We must add another consideration to the theory of variations or of continuity in policy: what were and what are the *objectives* of foreign policy under the Fifth Republic? Have there been variations in this regard? It appears to me that although the means have changed, and although the tactics employed have varied, there has been until now a rather noteworthy consistency in the objectives of foreign policy under the Fifth Republic. I would almost go so far as to say that one could take at random any statement of General de Gaulle or Mr. Couve de Murville at any moment since 1958, and one would find (with allowance for style and context) that the affirmation of objectives remains the same. For instance, on April 28, 1964, Mr. Couve de Murville stated before the National Assembly: "France has resumed her position in all sectors of world affairs."

If *"position"* is read as *rang* (rank), you will recognize the almost single-minded goal of foreign policy since 1958. The means selected in pursuit of that goal are apparent in the ambiguous objective of France's European policy: "To establish Europe as a power in itself, and not to dilute it in advance by immersing it in a wider conglomeration where it would immediately lose its personality." I say *ambiguous objectives of France's European policy* because (and this confusion has existed since 1958) Europe is considered both as a means for France to resume a status worthy of her historic mission, and, on the other hand, as a goal desirable in itself. Europe must one day come to have a status of its own.

France's purpose was to establish her independent status, especially in regard to the United States. But Europe's role in this conception was ambiguous. Europe was viewed both as an instrument of French national policy and as an objecti.e desirable in itself. Since 1958, there has also arisen the notion that "within both camps, conditions favor a return to pluralism." The rejection of integration, the importance attached to the "third world" as an objective and as a field of influence for French policy have likewise been dominant themes in the foreign policy of the Fifth Republic. I believe that there has been very solid continuity in the objectives of foreign policy.

The Results

I believe that the positive record is short, and the negative record very long. The credit side is relatively thin by comparison with the debit side of the tally sheet.

The Credit Tally. On the credit side: *prestige.* This is as noteworthy to the Frenchman considering French foreign policy as it is for the foreigner. There has rarely been more talk about French foreign policy; rarely has more attention been paid to the slightest word that leaves the tongue of a French statesman. General de Gaulle has certainly succeeded in acquiring prestige, and one might wonder whether prestige does not constitute an end in itself for General de Gaulle, independent of its use. Prestige may certainly be credited to the positive side of the balance sheet in that *French diplomacy receives much greater c nsideration in the "third world"* than it did in 1958. This is explained not only by the end of the Algerian War, but also by the Fifth Republic's policy of pluralism within the blocs and by the liberal attitude taken in regard to the internal regimes of the countries of the "third world."

Another positive credit falls in the domain of *l'Europe économique,* of common policies — notably agricultural policy.

Regarding Franco-German relations, *the record is mixed,* because on the one hand, the rapprochement begun under the Fourth Republic was reinforced and emphasized; but on the other hand, there is a growing difficulty in defining common policies because of different conceptions concerning Europe and the Atlantic Community.

Last on the credit side of the ledger is the freedom of action Mr. Couve de Murville spoke of in the National Assembly — not so much to reverse the fundamental decisions, but to be more free at every point; one might almost say more in one's choice of vocabulary than in political orientation.

The Debit Tally. When compared with this credit reckoning, however, the debits seem quite impressive. The *force de frappe:* in the security and diplomatic power that nuclear weapons are supposed to provide, the positive consequences in the foreseeable future appear meager to me. Of course, one can argue that a great deal of attention is being paid to French nuclear policy, but I believe that it can be safely said that the Big Two pay attention to French nuclear policy mainly because of its precedent for the dissemination of atomic weapons. It is not so much the French force in itself that troubles both Washington and Moscow, but the fact that this force does not conform to the policy of nondissemination of nuclear weapons, and thus creates a situation in the world diplomatic field that neither of the Big Two desires.

The result obtained is more an annoyance for world diplomacy than a reinforcement of French defense or diplomacy. Indeed, it does not appear that either now or in the foreseeable future the French nuclear force will truly serve as a *deterrent* — that it will be capable of discouraging a potential aggressor by itself. Nor does it appear that it will be capable of serving as a *detonator* of the American nuclear force; that is, to draw the United States into a conflict against its will. France's European allies align themselves with American nuclear strategy for the most part, so that France would stand alone in threatening to push the button. Germany, moreover, is topographically situated between the potential aggressor and France. But Germany is much closer to the United States than to

France in the domain of strategy. Consequently, the credibility of the French threat remains extremely weak. The power that the *force de frappe* was supposed to provide is perceptible neither in military discussions nor in international political discussions, and it does not appear that by 1970 the situation will have changed substantially.

On the other hand, the French *non*-nuclear force, which *could* conceivably lend considerable weight to French diplomacy within the Atlantic Alliance (in line with Atlantic policy, described earlier) is in the process of disappearing, because most of the military budget is allocated to the *force de frappe*. This means that French conventional forces constitute a weak contribution to NATO's global strategy, rendering less and less probable any reinforcement of French participation within NATO. There were two possibilities for France to acquire greater importance within the Alliance: (1) to constrain the United States and Great Britain, through the existence of the *force de frappe,* to create a sort of club of atomic powers within NATO. Every attempt at this since 1958 failed. Or, (2) within the framework of NATO strategy, to claim for France greater participation in integrated decisions based on the French contribution. This also failed.

The policy of the "empty chair" has been very widely practiced by the Fifth Republic, not only within NATO, but also at the Disarmament Conference in Geneva, or from time to time, at the United Nations. The goal is evident: to oblige others to take greater account of France through absence than they do when she is obliged to join in decisions over which she can exert no decisive influence. But until now, it could hardly be maintained that France's absence has very strongly impressed the others, or that that absence has considerably influenced their policies.

L'Europe politique is almost completely blocked. Responsibility is very divided: it is far from being entirely the fault of General de Gaulle and his Government. I believe that among the crucial factors involved, one must include the style adopted by General de Gaulle in his European policy. Despite the reticence and the serious obstacles to political unification among the five others, the French style of political pressure, and noncommunity behavior within the nascent community contributed to the difficulties and obstacles posed by others.

In the negative balance, one might also include the likelihood that the worldwide scope of General de Gaulle's policy will, in the end, lead to the predominance of Germany in Europe. But the diplomatic and political strength of a country are not measured solely by the quantity of its economic investments, and it so happens that the Federal Republic of Germany does not exist as an independent political subject in the international field. Chancellor Erhard's policy has until now consisted in getting along with everyone precisely by not taking any strong stands. In order for there to be leadership, or domination, there must be a policy. Now, for reasons which I indicated earlier, it is not conceivable for the time being that the Federal Republic would pursue a policy different from that of the United States. Consequently, there is no German domination of Europe. But there is indeed — and this is a setback in view of General de Gaulle's diplomatic objectives — an ever stronger American influence in European politics through the medium of German loyalty to United States policies.

Another consequence of the current policy of the Fifth Republic has been to push Germany toward nuclear rearmament, which is neither in line with the objectives of the Fifth Republic, nor in the interest of the Western Alliance as a whole. But the logic of French nuclear independence and of European nonintegration must ultimately lead to the nuclear rearmament of Germany, for there is no reason why Germany should renounce the last of its unrestored equalities if international relations among European nations are simply to be played out on the plane of "coordinated" nations.

Finally, one must mark on the debit side the sort of general irritation that General de Gaulle has aroused nearly everywhere. In reading the innumerable commentaries on the policies of the Fifth Republic in foreign countries, one is surprised at the extraordinary errors in analysis regarding the objectives and the means pursued by General de Gaulle. But a policy leading to such misunderstandings and such errors in analysis on the part of foreign partners must be held in some measure responsible for such distrust and incomprehension. *One is in some measure responsible for the image one creates in the eyes of others.* Now, the image created by the foreign policy of the Fifth Republic often corresponds very little to the objectives revealed by a serious analysis. But distrust of the objectives exists. There is much uneasiness regarding de Gaulle's ultimate motives, and if this be the case, it is because diplomatic style and content have not succeeded in dealing with the problem.

The Opposition

Foreign Incomprehension. Before examining the domestic opposition, a word on the incomprehension outside France concerning French goals. A few lines earlier, I said that the French Government was responsible to some extent for this misunderstanding, but there are aspects of this lack of understanding that stand quite independent of French policy. I should like to cite two examples: the German attitude concerning French policy toward the "third world" and the American attitude concerning what is called on the other side of the Atlantic "French nationalism."

On March 31, 1964, a very influential German daily, the *Frankfurter Allgemeine Zeitung,* published an article on the attitude of the French delegation in Geneva during the dicussions on world commerce, alleging that it was solely because of Gaullist isolationism that the French delegation made a number of proposals for the agenda. Now, if we examine these French proposals in Geneva, we note that they would receive the nearly unanimous approval of French experts — Gaullists and anti-Gaullists, without any distinction — because what is involved is a specific conception of international relations and of the laws of economics. In this regard, neither the United States nor Germany can understand that for the French, the "free laws of the market" are totally insufficient to solve the commercial and economic problems of the underdeveloped countries.

Another example. Senator Fulbright, Chairman of the Senate Foreign Relations Committee in the United States, wrote: "It is not between American hegemony and European independence that the

Western countries must choose, really; it is between an Atlantic association embracing all of the North Atlantic democracies, and the division of the West into a European community and a distinct and competing Anglo-Saxon community." And further on: "The concept of Atlantic association is supported by the fact that an international system founded on the unlimited sovereignty of the nation has become, in the nuclear age, an anachronism constituting an intolerable danger."[1]

Now, the United States is in a position at least as anachronistic as the anachronism France is allegedly guilty of. In constantly reproaching General de Gaulle for his refusal to submit to a majority vote, American opinion has displayed an altogether disarmingly clear conscience, in view of the American *inability* even to conceive of the fact that true Atlantic equality would require *American* submission to majority decisions. The incomprehension here is total, for American leaders and the American public find it inconceivable that the United States should lose its full sovereignty in matters of decision making.

The Opposition in France. The domestic opposition in France is striking in the first place because of its moderation: the moderate stance of the Communist Party currently is due to the cordial relations between Paris and Moscow. The other parties are moderate in their opposition because the vocabulary of independence is prestigious, and because to interfere with this prestige would appear to defend the absence of prestige under the Fourth Republic. But most important, even the domestic opposition agrees with de Gaulle's essential diplomatic objectives.

I have selected an example among the Leftist opposition — the furthest Left possible, except for the Communists, since one would assume at the start that there would be no violent objections on the Right to a policy appealing to the nation and to prestige. Toward mid-April, 1964, the members of the "socialist family" convened. Mr. Gérard Jacquet, former Minister, and political director of *Populaire,* declared: "We must recognize that so long as the tension between East and West has not disappeared, a politically united Eu-

[1] *Le Monde diplomatique,* March, 1964.

rope must remain within the Atlantic camp." In other words I, a member of the SFIO,[2] am obliged to sound like General de Gaulle: the Atlantic Alliance is necessary because of the East-West tension. But may East-West tension end at last so that there will no longer be any Atlantic Alliance! All the debates of the SFIO Left, and even further Left, turn about the issue of whether the Atlantic Alliance should be abandoned right away, or only after the East-West conflict has subsided. The principle of the independence of Europe is unanimously approved.

Where does the opposition differ with de Gaulle's diplomacy and objectives? Only over the *content* of this "Europe." But at the meeting of the "socialist family," this was most unclear. Similarly, in recognizing Communist China, General de Gaulle gave expression to what his most violent Leftist opponents were constantly demanding: detachment from the United States, and the formulation of a future policy independent of the policy of the two blocs which they hope to see disappear.

The reproach of inadequate support of the alliance with the United States and an insufficient contribution to the Atlantic alliance finds little sympathy in French public opinion. To plead in behalf of a more solid alliance with the United States and for greater integration within the Atlantic community is to come up against the rather deep reaction of anti-Americanism in France, and also to come up against the prestige of independence and the possibility, if I might say so, of saying "Nuts!" to the Americans.

What about Gaston Defferre?[3] I shall begin with the most important statement of his program — before the extraordinary national convention of the SFIO on February 2, 1964: "In foreign policy even more than in domestic policy, if Gaullist objectives are often well chosen, the method employed to achieve them is nearly always bad." What is criticized is the method, not the objectives: "De Gaulle has utilized a bad method to ensure French independ-

---

[2] *Translator's note: "Section Française de l'Internationale Ouvrière,"* or the French Socialist Party.

[3] The socialist mayor of Marseilles, who was a candidate for the presidency until June, 1965.

ence in choosing the military domain." The military domain is a bad domain, but to seek independence as a primary goal is a good goal. European policy is a failure, according to Defferre: "General de Gaulle has made Germany the arbiter of Europe. Now, while we desire Franco-German understanding, we do not want German domination of Europe."

The final goal, as defined by Mr. Defferre: "The putting into operation of a socialist type of policy throughout a continent developed industrially into the European nation, can, for the first time since the birth of the socialist idea in the world, bring about a new model of civilization, a model different from both modern American capitalism and Russian collectivism." Mr. Defferre then states that there must be an East-West rapprochement: "This rapprochement can give rise to a Europe whose new type of civilization will serve as a link between East and West."

Mr. Defferre is more "Third-Force Europe" than General de Gaulle, or General de Gaulle is more Atlantic-oriented than Gaston Defferre. At the same time, however, the concept of a "nation-Europe" is more "integrationist" than de Gaulle. There is a contradiction between the idea of a socialist Europe and this idea of a European nation. I once asked Willy Brandt what he thought of the socialist Europe of Mr. Defferre. He replied: "Please, let's not talk about that, for 'Socialist Europe' means to dismiss in advance the very strong nonsocialist currents in favor of European unification, and if we want a socialist Europe, we will not have [this kind of integrated] Europe." In his notion of a socialist "Europe" linking East and West, which neither the German socialists nor the English socialists desire (the former because they very much desire an Atlantic community, and the latter because they are opposed to European integration), Defferre is very much a utopian.

I could go on quoting Mr. Defferre. It seems to me that all his comments point in the same direction. The most important and meaningful parting of ways concerns European policy. I believe that the most well-balanced presentation of the policy of the Opposition was formulated in an article written by Mr. Maurice Faure, former Secretary of State for Foreign Affairs, and President of the Radical

Party.[4] I refer you to this article because he defines very courageously the difficulties involved in opposing de Gaulle's foreign policy, on the basis of prestige and national interest. He explains the difficulty over the admission of England combined with the creation of an integrated Europe, and notes especially (what seems to me full of common sense, but difficult to defend publicly) that there is no good solution to the mechanism of Atlantic decision making. It is only by much patience, many negotiations, many discussions, that a compromise solution will be arrived at, leaving a virtual monopoly over the final decision concerning nuclear weapons in the hands of the United States, but defining in advance and in common the conditions under which the American President may play the nuclear poker game. This kind of compromise solution is most reasonable, but also most difficult to defend in public discussions at the time of legislative or presidential elections. This is why there is so little apparent difference between General de Gaulle and his adversaries, why the major leaders of the opposition remain silent when there is a parliamentary debate over foreign policy.

But it must likewise be added that nearly everyone is caught up by the basic currents of thought that form public opinion and that weigh on the whole of French foreign policy.

The Basic Trends of French Opinion

A leader's freedom of decision in foreign policy is limited both by the situation (by the facts impinging on him from outside) and by what one might call the "cultural determinants" of foreign policy; deep-seated feelings, established traditions. I should like to consider four elements of this cultural force.

The Refusal to Think in Military Terms. I should hardly exaggerate in speaking of the infantile status of French public opinion in regard to military problems. We have little enthusiasm for nuclear issues. In contrast to the strong reactions that nuclear issues provoke in Germany or Britain, the indifference of the French is extremely curious. There is indeed a deep sentimental reaction against the

---

[4] *Le Monde,* January 31, 1964.

force de frappe, and an equally certain refusal to think about the very notion of national defense. Hearts beat faster at the Bastille Day parade, but the purpose or cost of military glory or prestige is never questioned.

If there were no *force de frappe,* would it be necessary to have more men in uniform? Would it be necessary to spend more for conventional forces? Reply: the consequences of the opposition's European and Atlantic positions are never evaluated as military expenditures. The policy of the opposition would be very costly for the budget, and would entail, notably, a longer period of military service for young Frenchmen than at present. But the common attitude in France is to refuse to examine the problems of national defense in depth.

Francocentrism. The second attitude is Francocentrism. I should like to limit consideration of this factor to a domain which, in appearance, has nothing to do with foreign policy, but which, actually, is involved — the attitude of French university professors toward the reform of the University.

In the summer of 1963, *Le Monde* published an excellent article by a professor at the Faculté des Sciences in Lille, and my suspicions on reading that article were confirmed by a consultation of his biography: this man had studied not only in France, but in Switzerland, in England, and in the United States — which makes him a very rare exception among French professors. His ideas on education in France were supported by comparisons with other countries. Now the excellence of French education is a dogma, even for those who are passionately critical when they examine only things French. This attitude roundly asserts that everything being done in France is detestable, but on the whole, it is far superior to what is being done everywhere else! And this outlook applies to foreign policy as well.

The horizon is extremely limited. There is an element of cultural imperialism that makes it difficult to conceive of extending aid to English-speaking African countries, for instance, even if (despite Raymond Cartier) the idea of aiding French-speaking African countries has won acceptance. If the French language is spoken, that is sufficient to merit receiving aid; but if they speak English, their cultural level is insufficient to warrant French aid.

Americanophobia. This Francocentrism, or distrust of foreign experience, is especially evident in the third trend: Americanophobia. It is most extraordinary to note the success of Étiemble's best-seller, *Parlez-vous franglais?,* not so much because of its linguistic aspects as because of the explosion of virulent anti-Americanism that it represents. The English may well reply, as they did in the excellent article in the *Observer,* entitled "Parlez-vous Englench?", by pointing out the pernicious penetration of French vocabulary into the English language as well. Étiemble touched a sore point. Indeed, even a man as well trained in political science and as reflective as Maurice Duverger explained in an interview, concerning his most recent book: "It must be said, it must be written — the sole near danger for Europe is American civilization.[5] There will be neither Stalinism nor communism in France. All that is a scarecrow that no longer frightens anyone but the sparrows. From 1946–48, in 1952, there was still a communist danger, but today all that appears past. In contrast, the pressure of American society, the domination of the American economy, the invasion of the American mentality — all that is very dangerous." I do not know very precisely what the American mentality is, but I feel rather close to those who replied to Étiemble — for instance, Pierre Daninos,[6] and particularly the most extraordinary commentary by Mr. Octave Gelinier in *Le Monde* of March 31: "Why we speak Franglais," in which he declares: "If we had invented the bulldozer, the twist, the mixer, these things would have French names."[7] He shows to what extent there is a sort of defensive reaction involved in not accepting a society founded on economic and industrial development, and that in the very basic anti-Americanism which exists in France, there is a sort of nostalgia for a bygone civilization.

This results in what I call "neutralism," for it is not a procommunist or antiliberal inclination, but a reaction of this sort: Ameri-

[5] *L'Express,* March 5, 1964.
[6] *Figaro,* April 4, 1964.
[7] *Le Monde,* March 31, 1964.

cans, Russians — each is as bad as the other in his own way. This is reminiscent of a popular story that made the rounds in 1949: Churchill, Stalin, and Truman went to Heaven, and were questioned by God-the-Father about the wish that they would most like to be granted. Stalin said: "I would like to see all the Americans wiped out." Truman said: "I would like to see all the Russians wiped out." — "And you, Churchill?" — "Oh, me, . . . just grant these two gentlemen their wishes."

A Particular Version of "Occidentalism." Thus, the French outlook can be characterized, to some extent, by what might be called an absence of Occidentalism within the Western alliance. I believe we must distinguish two consequences of this outlook: the one deplorable, and the other excellent. The first is a form of *double morality*. It is the idea that one must be extremely demanding, from a liberal point of view, in regard to the Western world, but not in regard to the East. To begin with, the East must be judged according to realism and not according to morality. One must understand Khrushchev when he accepted the building of the Berlin wall or even when he ordered the workers of Budapest to be shot at: he had no choice. But if the Americans should decide to take action in Cuba, this is not because they had no choice, but rather because they are ignoble. This judgment, based on realism in the one case and on morality in the other, results in a double standard of morality. But there is, in addition, an even more basic issue: we learned in our schoolbooks that there is good violence and there is bad violence — depending on whether it is used in the interest of progress or reaction. Hence, when the rights of man are flaunted, on the other side of the iron curtain, where by definition progress reigns, it is not at all the same as a similar occurrence in Angola or in Algeria.

For example, Étienne Mougeotte, who was a vice-president of UNEF,[8] declared in an article concerning his attendance at a meeting of the International Student Union: "We took care to present our position in one single speech, in order to avoid an ideological debate at all costs. We were commissioned by the general assembly

[8] *Translator's note: UNEF, L'Union Nationale des Étudiants Français,* means the National Union of French Students.

of UNEF to recall our attachment to two principles: the struggle
for peace and disarmament, and the support of students struggling
for national liberation." It goes without saying that in his view, national liberation is a notion that applies only to the underdeveloped
countries of the "third world," and which cannot possibly apply to
countries east of the iron curtain. He adds: "The unity of the student movement can only be realized on concrete bases. The struggle
for peace, support in the struggle for national liberation, the de-
mocratization of education are principles that might serve in the
building of such unity."[9]

At no time is there any question of the right to truth and to intellectual freedom, claimed by the Grenoble Charter of UNEF, for this
theme is not appropriate to discussions of the International Student
Union. The issue will be raised in regard to Angola, but not in regard to the Soviet Union, or still less in regard to East Germany.
There are two standards of morality: the one serving to criticize the
West, the other serving to dismiss the criticisms regarding the East.
This double standard of morality runs very deep in French public
opinion, and explains why, in contrast to the Americans or the Germans, France does not feel itself much committed to the Western
world. Paradoxically, this detachment is justified in the name of
liberal principles.

But of course, there is another side to the issue: the French are
much more sensitive to the inconsistencies in Western liberalism
than other Western countries are. It is very striking, in this regard,
to note the difference between the reactions of the French press —
from Left to Right — to events in Brazil, and those of the German
or American press. From Right to Left, the French press reacted by
noting: "If the Americans seek to spread communism in Brazil,
they are on the right road — they have only to continue considering
as communist any government that attempts to react against the
injustice of social structures and the absurdities of Brazilian economic life."

This impression that American policy is blind to the quasi-so-
cialist needs of underdeveloped countries seeking to transform their

[9] *UNEF Review,* March 21–27, 1964.

present structures, explains still more the French determination to avoid alignment in a sort of permanent "occidentalism." Once again, this goes back very far: the American Revolution was basically liberal — there was no Convention or French-style Terror in the United States. The French have learned that the Terror does not necessarily last forever — and this may lead them to underestimate the horror of violence in the name of progress, but it likewise leads them to understand that change ought not necessarily to be judged according to a violence that might be only passing. This is the other element of difference between French opinion and the notion of a "Western world."

A Foreign Policy: For What Purpose?

We must distinguish here between attitudes and action. If you reflect upon the reasons why Gaullism has met such success in France, notably in foreign policy, I believe that the conclusion must be: because it brings prestige cheap, because General de Gaulle alone defines his policies, because he does not invite the participation of the French people other than by the confidence he demands of them. The result is marvellous for French citizens: they are invited to be spectators of French prestige achieved by a single man. When they *are* asked to participate by a sacrifice, the result is hostility to the *force de frappe* and *"Cartiérisme."*

In its devotion to prestige — winning diplomatic status and presence without basic consequences in the individual life of the citizen — Gaullism represents a nearly optimum solution for foreign policy. One feels prestigious, while remaining a spectator. One must inquire to what extent foreign policy *can* have well-defined objectives. Mr. Couve de Murville recently sang the praises of France's recovery of freedom of action. This was in itself an ultimate objective, but freedom of action in order to obtain what? This is a difficult question: is it simply in order to act in the international field? To increase the prosperity of French citizens? But the prosperity of French citizens might be increased even more if there were not such a broad range of activity in the international field — if

France looked to Switzerland as a model, rather than to the United States. I am not certain whether, if given the choice between prestige and personal well-being, the French citizen would not prefer the latter. Is this ignoble? According to what standard? What is the value of prestige, anyway?

Prestige, the Nation, solidarity with the whole of mankind: in the name of what morality or choice can one contend that the prestige of France is the most important goal, rather than the evolution of world society? There is, of course, a means of reconciling the two, which amounts to saying that since France is France, all that she does contributes to the progress of mankind — this may be a consolation, but, at the very least, it remains to be demonstrated as a postulate. There are no answers to these questions. In his book, *Peace and War among Nations,* Raymond Aron outlines the difficulty, in pointing out that all states have a multiplicity of objectives. But to maintain that there is a multiplicity of objectives (well-being, prestige, international society) does not stipulate on what basis the citizen should judge, for better or for worse, the foreign policy that is pursued in his name.

I have no solution to offer. I wish simply to make one remark in conclusion: it is striking to note to what degree any discussion of French foreign policy — whether under the Fourth or Fifth Republic — always results in a debate over the ultimate purpose of that policy. What results do we hope to obtain through foreign policy? Is French foreign policy intended to serve the interest of the individual French citizen? the nation? international society? Consequently, the debate over foreign policy, both in Parliament and in the press, ends up going around in circles. If General de Gaulle's foreign policy encounters very few valid criticisms, in the final analysis, this is because what is criticized is not the fundamental basis of his foreign policy, but only its forms. The means used in pursuit of the goal of national power, or national influence, are challenged, but not the goal itself. Once the power of the nation and the influence of the purely national community are accepted as the ultimate objectives of foreign policy, one may well criticize the means, but he has already affirmed his approval of the major choices.

Is national society itself its own supreme goal? Is the ultimate purpose of foreign policy the reinforcement of the nation's power? It is the questioning of these postulates that would really open the way for a national debate over the foreign policy of the Fifth Republic.

AND NOW . . .

The world has not remained immobile during the past two years. Khrushchev has been deposed; President Johnson has scored a triumphant victory at the polls; Communist China has become an atomic power; Chancellor Erhard has succeeded Adenauer, but lost his prestige; Ben Bella has been expelled from power by Colonel Boumedienne; and the United States has become more deeply involved in the war in Vietnam. In France, General de Gaulle received only 43.7 per cent of the votes on the first ballot in the 1965 presidential elections, and was re-elected for seven years on December 19, 1965 by 54.5 percent of those voting on the second ballot. De Gaulle's relative setback in the first round was partly due to his European policy. This fact was evident in the surprising success of Lecanuet, the candidate who opposed the General in the name of European integration — attacking the French position since June 30, 1965.

The year 1964 had ended on a note of optimism in Brussels: a decision had just been reached concerning the fourth stage in agricultural policy, and it appeared decisive. On June 30, 1960 the Commission of the European Economic Community, headed by Hallstein, completed its work on a final text outlining the Commission's proposals concerning the drafting and the entering into force of the common agricultural policy. On January 14, 1962 the EEC Council (composed of the foreign ministers of the member states) adopted six regulations governing certain products and groups of products, leading gradually to a common organization of markets; and the regulation governing the financing of the common agricultural policy. On December 23, 1963 the Council approved regulations governing the gradual organization of a common market in rice, beef, and dairy products, and issued directives concerning the coming Kennedy Round on tariffs and trade to the Commission. And on December 15, 1964, again after difficult negotiations, the Council made fundamental decisions concerning the price of cereals, agreed on a common market for pork products, eggs, and poultry; and defined the functions of the European Fund for Agricultural Orientation and Guarantee.

But as early as the spring of 1965, new difficulties could be seen. In order to finance the common agricultural policy, the Commission proposed a system that would give the Community important resources of its own, and likewise bolster the powers of the European Parliament. The French Government saw in this an attempt to step up political integration, contrary to the French position. It appears that this was the main reason why Couve de Murville, then presiding officer of the Council, closed the meeting of June 30, devoted to financial policy, on a note of failure. Nor was it merely a temporary difficulty; for General de Gaulle had decided to pursue an "empty-chair" policy in Brussels so long as he had not obtained satisfaction on two points: a reduction in the Commission's activity, and an unspecified moratorium on the articles of the Treaty dealing with the entry into force of the system of majority decision. From July 6 on, France no longer participated in the work of the Council or the Commission, apart from the application of regulations already in force. On September 9, General de Gaulle spelled out at a press conference one of his conditions for furthering European construction: the abandonment of the provision for majority rule, which was supposed to enter into force with the third stage of the Common Market on January 1, 1966.

On January 30, 1966, after France had agreed to talks between the Six, the ministers decided on a "return to the work of the Community, according to normal procedures," despite the differences which continued to exist, and which were clearly set forth:

> In the event of decisions that can be adopted by majority on the proposal of the Commission, when very important interests of one or several partners are at stake, the members of the Council will attempt, within a reasonable period of time, to arrive at solutions that could be adopted by all members of the Council in respect of their mutual interests and those of the Community, in accordance with Article 2 of the Treaty.
>
> With regard to the preceding paragraph, the French delegation considers that, when very important interests are concerned, discussion must be continued until agreement has been reached.

The six ministers agreed without difficulty on the questions raised in the French *aide-mémoire* concerning the Commission's "behavior" — practical arrangements for cooperation, not affecting the "respective powers and duties of the two institutions," were defined by the Council regarding its relationship with the Commission. But these arrangements did not go so far as the French proposals.

The Luxemburg agreements made possible the resumption of negotiations on agriculture. On May 11, 1966 the Six agreed on the financing of agricultural policy until 1970. They decided that as of July 1, 1968 there would be free circulation of all agricultural and industrial products within the EEC. On July 24, new regulations on sugar, milk, fruit, and vegetables were adopted, and the existing regulations were altered so that *L'Europe verte,* or the common agricultural market, could become a reality.

The facts are easy to record. But to interpret them from the point of view of French foreign policy is more difficult. The intense pressure placed on France's five partners during the second half of 1965 was not very effective in that it culminated merely in a unilateral declaration concerning majority vote, and in restrictions of little consequence imposed on the Commission. Why then the hard line in 1965 and the more flexible stance in 1966? It seems that the break on June 30 was primarily due to Couve de Murville's annoyance with his partners, who were unwilling to carry out the en-

gagements they had made earlier regarding financial regulations —
or, more precisely, their desire to link the execution of their promises
with progress toward *l'Europe politique*. Once the break had been
made, the French Government sought to exploit the situation for its
own purposes, and it failed. In the first place, France did not succeed
in splitting the Five; none of its efforts at bilateral negotiations
(notably with Italy) succeeded. Second, France had too much interest in the building of the common agricultural market. It must not
be forgotten that 46.5 per cent of the arable land within the EEC
lies in France (comparel with 28.4 per cent in Italy, 19.4 per cent
in Germany, and 5.7 per cent in the Benelux countries). In relation
to this vast area, France is, of the Six, the country with the smallest
population to feed. Because of this, her logical role appears to be
that of making up for the agricultural deficit of her partners. Moreover, France has the largest average arable land surface per farmer,
7.8 hectares. This situation, combined with the fact that the average
size of French farms (15.2 hectares) is the largest in the Community, helps to give France great potential in obtaining better
costs of production. France will, consequently, find herself confronted more and more with the vital problem of foreign outlets,
and the policy of guiding production and organizing the markets on
the European scale can indeed intensify or resolve that problem.

Finally, the presidential elections doubtless were decisive. General
de Gaulle realized that the break in Brussels had met with the disapproval of all organized groups, from agricultural associations to
labor unions, including the industrial sector. Indeed, his decision
affords a very interesting theoretical case for historians and political
scientists: a determined leader can perfectly well resist all efforts
made by pressure groups to influence his policy; political will does
not necessarily take economic interests into account. But de Gaulle
had probably not thought that "Europe" would provide a very
profitable issue for the opposition during the electoral campaign.
After the presidential elections, he drew a lesson for the forthcoming
legislative elections scheduled for the spring of 1967. The Luxemburg agreements completely disarmed the "European" opposition,
and indeed all opposition in the domain of foreign policy; for his

dramatic decision to withdraw from the Atlantic Alliance was not at all unpopular.

On April 14, 1966, Couve de Murville declared in the National Assembly:

> Every time, for the past six years, that we have together discussed measures to take toward what is generally called the political Europe, everyone has always taken the stand that defense was a taboo subject: that is NATO's business. As for international policy, doubtless one could be bold enough to discuss it a little bit, but the really appropriate forum was, nevertheless, that of NATO.
>
> If there are really two contradictory concepts — and I am intentionally going to use an expression that is not ours — they are those of European integration and of Atlantic integration.
>
> In the final analysis, it involves a change in the relations between America and Europe.[1]

Thus presented, the decisions reached in March could hardly shock large sectors of public opinion. Their broad outlines had already been announced at the press conference on February 21. The themes were not new, even though certain expressions were. The Treaty of April 4, 1949 remains valid, but the "measures for implementation taken subsequently" no longer corresponded to what France deemed satisfactory, in that the evolution of the communist bloc countries reduced the threat which existed "at the time when the American protectorate was set up in Europe under the cover of NATO." Integration can no longer be justified, since the Soviet Union can destroy the United States, "which has made the decisions of the Americans as to the eventual use of their bombs at least indeterminate." Moreover, "the conflicts" the United States is involved in other parts of the world threaten to unleash a general war in which NATO "would be automatically involved . . . even when it would not have so desired."

Lastly, France's determination to dispose of herself, a determination without which she would soon cease to believe in her own

---

[1] For all quotations from the important debates of April 13, 14, 19, and 20, cf. *Journal Officiel. Assemblée nationale,* for April 14, 15, 20, and 21.

role and be able to be useful to others, is incompatible with a defense organization in which she finds herself subordinate.

Consequently, without going back on her adherence to the Atlantic Alliance, France is going, between now and the final date set for her obligations, which is April 4, 1969, to continue to modify successively the measures currently practiced, insofar as they concern her.

General de Gaulle wrote to President Johnson on March 7, 1966 stating:

> Our Atlantic Alliance will reach the end of its first stage in three years. I should like you to know that France is aware of the extent to which the solidarity in defense thus established among the fifteen Western peoples helps to guarantee their security — and especially the essential role of the United States of America in that task. Therefore, France resolves, as of now, to remain a party to the treaty signed in Washington on April 4, 1949. This means that, unless the events of the next three years should alter the fundamental basis of East-West relations, France is determined in 1969 and thereafter, as well as today, to fight alongside the Allies in the event that one of them should be the victim of an unprovoked aggression.
>
> France considers, however, that the changes effected or in process since 1949 in Europe, in Asia, and elsewhere — as well as the evolution of her own situation and forces — no longer justify, insofar as she is concerned, the military arrangements made after the conclusion of the Alliance, including both multilateral conventions and special agreements between the French and American governments.
>
> This is why France intends to restore within her territory the full exercise of her sovereignty, currently modified by the permanent presence of Allied military forces, or by the use made of her air space — to end her participation in the integrated command, and no longer to place her forces at the disposal of NATO.

The text of the *aide-mémoire,* delivered to all the Allied governments on March 11, is more precise and more brusque. After a similar elaboration of France's motives, it continues:

> Doubtless, it would have been conceivable for negotiations to be

undertaken to amend the provisions in force by common agreement. The French Government would have been happy to propose it, had it been given to believe that such negotiations could lead to the outcome that the French Government itself has in view. Unfortunately, everything shows that such an undertaking would be doomed to failure, since France's partners appear to be, or assert that they are all advocates of maintaining the status quo, or else of strengthening everything which, from the French viewpoint, appears henceforth unacceptable.

France is therefore led to draw, insofar as she is concerned, the consequences of the situation, that is, to take for herself the measures that appear to her necessary and that, in her view, are in no way incompatible with her participation in the alliance, or with her participation, should the need arise, in military operations at the side of her allies.

Already, in the past, the French Government took measures in the direction involved for its naval forces assigned to NATO, either in the Mediterranean or in the Atlantic.

The question now is the ground and air forces stationed in Germany and assigned to allied command in Europe. France proposes to put an end to that assignment. The decision will entail her simultaneous withdrawal from the two integrated commands under which those forces fall and in which she participates in the NATO framework, namely the Supreme Command Allied Forces Europe and the Central Europe Command, and it will thereby entail the transfer of the headquarters of these two commands outside of French territory.

After raising the issue of the French forces in Germany, the *aide-mémoire* concludes on a discreetly threatening note:

The French Government is, furthermore, prepared to enter into a discussion on the military facilities that could be made available to the Canadian Government on French territory in the event of a conflict in which both countries would participate by virtue of the Atlantic alliance. These facilities could be the subject of an agreement to be concluded between the two Governments.

At the end of the month, a "timetable" was submitted, setting July 1, 1966 as the date for withdrawing French forces in Germany

from the allied command. On July 23, all French military personnel
and auditors were to be withdrawn from the NATO College:

> The withdrawal of the French elements assigned to the allied
> general staffs (Supreme Command and Allied Forces Central
> Europe), as well as to the NATO College, entails the transfer of
> the headquarters of these bodies outside of French territory.
>
> Consequently, the French Government, by virtue of Article 16
> of the protocol of August 28, 1952 on the status of the General
> Headquarters, is going to notify the United States Government of
> the denunciation of this protocol, which will cease to be in force
> on March 31, 1967.

The various American responses insisted on the absence of consultation, on the fact that several of the denounced agreements stipulated that they remained in force for the duration of the treaty, and
on the link between the integrated command organization and the
Paris Agreements of 1954 concerning the status of Germany (whose
validity the French notes affirmed). But rather than the American
reaction, which is well known to the American reader, it will be
more useful to outline the arguments in the debate in French circles.
A motion of censure was indeed submitted by certain leaders of the
opposition, and this was discussed for four days in the National
Assembly. The text of the motion read, in part:

> Noting that the President of the Republic has decided to with-
> draw French forces from NATO without consulting either the
> Government or the French Parliament, and without entering into
> negotiations with our allies;
>
> Considering, on the one hand, that in the absence of a positive
> alternative policy — notably concerning European policy — this
> decision leaves France isolated and thereby creates a dangerous
> situation for our country;
>
> That it leads the Government to intensify the nationalist char-
> acter of its defense policy, and notably its effort to develop an au-
> tonomous *force de frappe*.

First of all, we must point out that this motion received only 137
votes, whereas 242 would have been required to defeat the Government.

The major criticisms were summed up by René Pleven, former President of the Council and author of the plan for a European Army in 1950; by the Socialist leaders Guy Mollet and Gaston Defferre; and by Maurice Faure, former Secretary of State in charge of Foreign Affairs, and negotiator of the Treaties of Rome creating the Common Market and Euratom. These men are leaders of the Center-Left and the Left.

René Pleven first attacked the method used — the decision to withdraw French forces left no room for discussion.

> Neither at home, where the French people are expected merely to take note and to remain calm; nor abroad, where the Allies are called upon to carry out the decisions . . . and to pack up. In one year, you expect the place to be cleaned up!
>
> The method of the *fait accompli,* alas! we French have known and experienced all too well over the past 35 years. Coming from a country like France, which has contributed so greatly to the setting up of a certain world order and international law, such a method is surprising and shocking. The example we have given is dangerous and deplorable.
>
> To be sure, one might think that "Realpolitik" can dispense with gratitude and sentiment. But I doubt, Mr. Prime Minister, that a truly realistic policy can, in our time, flaunt the profound desires of the people; and in this case I doubt that it is wise for France to destroy little by little her capital of esteem, confidence, and friendship . . . to ruin, I would say, this capital of esteem, confidence, and friendship which our country has built up over two centuries in America.

And he continued:

> Our friend will depart without anything having been settled with the Soviets, without Russian forces having pulled out of a single inch of territories where their presence is hardly desired — consider, for one, Poland or Hungary. . . .
>
> Thus, the Americans will leave France; but ten years after Poznan, ten years after Budapest, the Russians do not budge. . . .
>
> But even supposing a Sino-American conflict should break out in Asia, why should NATO be involved, when the zone covered

by the treaty includes only Europe and the North Atlantic? Was
NATO drawn into the Korean War? When we ourselves were
involved in Indo-China NATO was not in the least drawn into
the conflict.

And since you keep repeating that the atomic force has only a
dissuasive power; that since Russia has developed nuclear weapons
capable of striking the United States directly, the United States
will no longer use its weapons to defend is allies; then how can
you claim at the same time that, because of fear of reprisals, the
United States will not use its weapons to defend Europe, but that
it will use them to defend South Vietnam or to attack China?

Guy Mollet concluded that the "most serious guarantee of the
American involvement, and therefore of no aggression within
Europe, lies in the physical presence of the Americans on our continent." Maurice Faure seconded that idea: "The French Government demands the withdrawal of American troops from France. If
all our European partners in NATO acted similarly, what American
forces would remain on the continent? . . . If the Atlantic Pact had
existed in 1940, the situation would certainly have been better; but
if NATO had existed, there would have been no war."

But in the eyes of the majority as well as part of the opposition —
and, as we shall see, in the public opinion — these arguments held
much less weight than those of the Government, set forth by Foreign
Minister Maurice Couve de Murville and Premier Georges Pompidou. This was true in regard both to the explicit arguments set forth,
and to those subsidiary arguments which were never thoroughly
developed, but which were important. One which recurs continually
in official declarations is the following: the Cuban crisis of 1962
demonstrated that the USSR recognizes the absolute superiority of
the United States, which in turn guarantees the security of Europe.
The Prime Minister traced the evolution of the Soviet Union from
the time of the Cuban crisis. It was likewise the Cuban crisis, which,
for the Foreign Minister, proved the effectiveness of dissuasion.[2]
Consequently, the integrated organization is no longer justified —

[2] See Chapter VII.

nor the subordination of France, which it implies. In fact, NATO is
totally dominated by the United States. Premier Pompidou declared:

> . . . Now, nothing better illustrates the accuracy of our theses and
> the totally illusory nature of the apparent equality within the
> Council than this affair of the strategic concept. For the strategy
> approved by the Council was that of massive and immediate atom-
> ic retaliation. Officially, it remains the NATO doctrine, and the
> Council has never been in a position to adopt a new strategic con-
> cept. But, in actual fact, this strategic concept approved by the
> NATO Council, unanimously, still theoretically in effect, has been
> abandoned by the Supreme Command in favor of the concept of
> the flexible response. It sufficed for Mr. McNamara to renounce
> Mr. Dulles' concepts for a strategy that the NATO Council had
> never approved to become, in fact, that of the Command. Cer-
> tainly, we protested; we refused to take part in the exercises that
> were too obviously based on that new theory; we discussed —
> "negotiated," as M. Pleven would like — that is, we upheld,
> throughout conferences of military leaders and diplomatic repre-
> sentatives, our theses conforming to the official NATO doctrine.
> The entire apparatus, nonetheless, obeyed the directives of the
> American Government. And I affirm, without violating secrets,
> that a large part, perhaps even the majority of allied military
> leaders, share our viewpoint. But as soon as the discussion be-
> comes public, not one of our allies contradicts the sovereign
> thesis of the United States. And this is what integration is,
> Mr. Pleven.

And such integration represents a great danger for European countries, particularly for France:

> But I will first of all mention one little fact. It relates to the Cuban
> affair. Faced with the threat weighing on the United States, Presi-
> dent Kennedy took immediate steps. He did not consult us but
> informed us, quickly, although after the fact. I point this out here
> only because you spoke of our policy of the *fait accompli*. We
> agreed with President Kennedy. But, even before we announced
> our position — while the NATO forces were supposed to be out-
> side the conflict, and while, even if they had been advised to take
> precautionary measures, no coded alert system had been set up —

the American forces in Europe, including those in France, had been placed in a state of alert and, I might add, alert of the highest degree.

For I ask that we please have the intellectual honesty not to claim to have answered when they say that nothing in NATO obliges us to enter into war automatically because one of our allies would have done so on his own in some part of the world: If one day there should really occur, for interests that would be alien to France and to her obligations in the alliance, a conflict between the United States and the USSR — and this is really the issue — who can maintain that the fact of having on our soil the American general headquarters in Europe, with its communications network and its entire command apparatus, not to mention air bases and supply depots, would not constitute an obvious and serious risk for us? Nothing in all that forces us to declare war, I admit, but all that could make us a target for atomic bombs, and is that not what is involved?

The reasoning is clear. An error in calculation on the part of the United States in Vietnam could lead to a war between the United States and China — an error which could lead to a confrontation with the USSR. We would then find ourselves faced with a Russian aggression provoked by the United States — a situation which, according to President Johnson's letter, does not call the Alliance into action. But since the two super-powers will avoid destroying one another, there is a risk that they will instead seek to strike one another wherever their troops are present outside their own territory — notably in Europe.

The counter-argument: "If all the European governments were to follow the same line . . ." remains largely hypothetical, partly because of Germany's position. The Germans are staunch partisans of the physical presence of the United States. Consequently, France remains protected by the direct protection given West Germany, and can therefore demand withdrawal from her own territory.

The French decision met with extreme irritation on Bonn, and this was evident in the legal difficulties surrounding the status of the French forces in Germany. A distinction must be drawn between the troops stationed in Berlin, and the divisions stationed within the territory of the Federal Republic. When a French soldier or officer takes the train from Berlin to Frankfurt, he changes, so to speak, his legal status between his departure and his arrival. In the former capital, he is an occupier, in conformity with the Four-Power agreements of 1944–45. He is, of course, there to protect the West Berliners, but this is a task based on his status as a member of the occupation forces. There is no German sovereignty, and no German military force in Berlin. In Frankfurt or in the Black Forest, on the other hand, the French soldier is an ally of the Bundeswehr, and his role is defined by the Paris Agreements, signed on October 23, 1954 and in force since May 5, 1955. Since the French forces in Berlin do not depend on NATO, their status is not affected by General de Gaulle's decision.

But it was obvious that once de Gaulle announced his break with NATO, the 1954 agreements would be subject to question — and especially, that the viewpoint expressed in the French *aide-mémoire* of March 29 would be unacceptable to the Germans. The text read: "The French forces will remain in Germany by virtue of the convention of October 23, 1954 governing the presence of foreign forces within the territory of the Federal Republic of Germany." It is true that this convention, which is unbelievably long and detailed (Article 46 alone, which deals with special privileges relating to hunting and fishing on West German territory, contains six extremely detailed paragraphs!), contains no reference to NATO. But, as the German note of May 3 pointed out, its text is inseparable from the other documents signed at the same time — between France and the Federal Republic, between the members of the Western European Union (the Six plus Great Britain), or between the members of the Atlantic Alliance. Most of these documents do specifically refer to the Atlantic Alliance. The German Government therefore concluded that "Once the French forces stationed within the territory of the Federal Republic withdraw from the Allied Command in Europe, without the accord of the other members of the Atlantic Alliance, France can no longer exercise her right to station troops, which is derived from the convention. . . ."

This conclusion is not incontestable, for it does not take into account the ambiguous character of the whole organization in 1954. The goal was to restore the sovereignty of the Federal Republic and equality of rights toward the Western countries, at the same time maintaining the special privileges of the United States, Great Britain, and France in relation to the fourth major power of 1945. The Three managed both to preserve their right to station troops in Germany and to renounce that privilege. Their troops were henceforth to be present because the Germans desired them to be. But their concern with 1945 was no less important than their concern with NATO.

German leaders were not unaware of this fact, since, in the Bonn Government's note, two quite different points were tied together. On the one hand, there was the idea of sovereignty and quality — the 1954 convention already represented substantial progress in that direction for the Germans, in comparison to the 1952 convention (which never entered into force because it was tied to the EDC). But it likewise reflected the unilateral character of the relations between the Federal Republic and the Three. Today, all new agreements must be based on total reciprocity. Even if no German troops are stationed in France, it must be understood that were German troops eventually to be stationed there, they would operate under the same legal conditions as the French troops stationed in Germany. Between the lines, one must read: Why should we be any less touchy about our sovereignty than you are in regard to the United States? On the other hand, there is the notion of strategic justification. The only reason for your presence is if it contributes to our common defenses. Give us guarantees that will assure us that, even if you pull out of NATO, you will still remain tied to us; that you are not planning to use your forces in Germany to put pressure on us. The position of the French Government until now can be summed up as follows: we aren't asking for anything. In other words, it is up to you if you want our troops to remain. If your answer is "Yes," it is because they are of some use to you. If they are of use to you, tell us what price you are prepared to pay for their presence.

This strategy seems finally to have paid off, since all that happened on July 1, 1966 was that General Köhler was named "Beauftrager

bei den Streitkräften Frankreichs in der Bundesrepublik" — i.e.,
representative of German sovereignty assigned to French forces.
After much hesitation, Chancellor Erhard expressed his desire that
the French troops remain; and the upshot was that legal arrangements were made — at a time when the United States and Great
Britain, for financial reasons or because of the demands of the war
in Vietnam, were reducing in number or in quality their own forces
stationed on German soil.

Since the Franco-German treaty was signed on January 22, 1963,
relations between France and Germany have been paradoxical. On
the one hand, the two countries continue along the road of rapprochement and interpenetration. In trade, each is the other's best
customer. In 1965 alone, 19.7 per cent of France's exports went to
the Federal Republic, and 19 per cent of her imports came from
across the Rhine. Germany's purchases within France have increased by 77 per cent in four years. The Franco-German Youth
Office has been a complete success, and the youth of both countries
— from all parts of the country and from all social classes — meet
by hundreds of thousands. Finally, the meetings between the leaders
provided for in the treaty have taken place as scheduled. On July
22, 1966 General de Gaulle made his seventh visit to Bonn. But on
the other hand, the general atmosphere continued to deteriorate
until de Gaulle's trip to the Soviet Union.

Since that time, there has been some improvement, which is reflected in Chancellor Erhard's speech on the occasion of de Gaulle's
visit on July 22:

> I do not wish to let this moment go by without expressing once
> again the gratitude of the German people for the position you
> took during your trip to Moscow, when you rejected the concept
> of the existence of two German states — thus refusing to recog-
> nize the existence of the "Soviet occupation zone." This was a
> precious assistance in defending our right to be the only spokes-
> man for Germany, and not to recognize the artificial creation of
> the occupation zone.
>
> I told you last January that we looked forward to your trip to
> Moscow with hope and interest, but without apprehension. The

German people have confidence in you, and you have justified
that trust.

What explains de Gaulle's position in Moscow? The Soviets
had no real interest in discussions with him unless he was in a position to promise German concessions. Just what is de Gaulle's viewpoint on the German problem, beyond the forthright statement at
his press conference on February 4, 1965? "It must be recognized,
first of all by Germany, that any settlement of which it would be
the subject would necessarily imply a settlement of its frontiers
and of its armaments, in agreement with all its neighbors, those on
the East and those on the West."

There are, first of all, the texts. In referring to the Paris agreements of 1954 governing the stationing of our troops in Germany,
could the French Government really consider the common declaration of the United States, Great Britain, and France, which was also
a part of those agreements, as no longer valid? This declaration
states:

> They consider the Government of the Federal Republic as the
> sole German Government freely and legitimately founded, and
> capable in that respect of speaking in the name of Germany as
> representative of the German people in international affairs.

Then comes the argument advanced by General de Gaulle in
Moscow: the German Democratic Republic does not exist legiti-
mately, because it is founded not on national consent, but on the
will of a foreign power. One must also add, doubtless, a sort of
sentimental reaction on de Gaulle's part. The two Germanies of
today correspond very well to the good and the bad Germany of the
traditional French image. On the one hand, Rhineland and Bavaria;
on the other, Prussia. Just as for many Germans, anticommunism is
facilitated by anti-Slav sentiment, so for General de Gaulle, hostility
toward communist Germany is very likely reinforced by an old
anti-Prussian prejudice.

But none of these reasons would appear convincing, if there were
not another much more directly connected with the over-all policies
of the General. To recognize the German Democratic Republic

would amount to accepting the status quo in Europe. Does not progress toward the reunification of Germany mean progress toward the reunification of the whole continent? But the General must also have realized that although Bonn desired the former and Bucharest the latter, neither had the slightest possibility of bringing this about in the near future for one very simple and compelling reason: nothing can be done without the two major powers, and they do not want to do anything.

The United States and the Soviet Union both have a vested interest in seeing that things do not change substantially in Europe, that the demarcation line between the two zones of influence remains sharply delineated. And if the last bone of contention between them — West Berlin — could be transplanted to another planet, Mr. Kosygin and President Johnson would probably find only advantages in that fact. General de Gaulle probably believed that by leaving out the United Staes, temporarily at least, he could persuade the Soviet Union to agree to a change. But that was not to be. Is it then in the interest of France to continue to promote the reunification of Germany? It appears to be indispensable in the broad view of de Gaulle's policies. In order to guarantee peace, and still more, the privileged position of France on the continent, the Federal Republic must not acquire atomic weapons. But the power of West Germany could lead to that possibility, especially in view of France's refusal of military and political integration, which encourages nationalist claims. To impose a discriminatory regime on the Federal Republic is becoming more and more difficult, and moreover is not even desirable since our goal is to maintain friendly relations with Germany. The renunciation must therefore be voluntary. And it will only be voluntary so long as there is some advantage to counterbalance it. This advantage is the hope of reunification.

If the division of Germany were to be accepted as permanent, and the Federal Republic were to consider itself as a permanent state with definite borders, the West German Government would be obliged to act on the basis of its power alone, and to claim atomic equality along with equal rights across the board. But once the

Federal Republic became a nuclear power, all hope of Moscow's agreeing to German unity would vanish.

Germany's hope for reunification thus fits in with the interests of French policy at present. What about reunification itself? If by some chance it were to become a reality (in keeping with present French policy), would not France be faced with the threat of domination by a Germany with a population of 70 million people? That would not happen, for reunification could only take place under the conditions set forth by General de Gaulle at his press conference on February 4, 1965. In other words, a reunified Germany would have only limited sovereignty, at least in military matters, and this limitation would provide France with compensation for Germany's demographic and industrial superiority.

General de Gaulle's visit to the Soviet Union from June 20 to July 1, 1966 marked the climax in the rapprochement begun in 1963. The main cause of this rapprochement must be found in the failure of his German policy — slow deterioration until late 1964, more obvious and accelerated in 1965 and 1966. It is difficult to say when, exactly, the head of state realized his mistake, i.e., that the Federal Republic, much more than Great Britain, was the United States's "Trojan Horse" in Europe. At any rate, it was before Ludwig Erhard came into office, probably when the Bundestag unanimously voted a resolution intended to be used as a preamble to the law authorizing the ratification of the Franco-German Treaty. The text, by apparently innocuous statement, showed in fact that the Federal Republic did not intend to follow General de Gaulle. The 1963 failure marked the turning point in the foreign policy of the Fifth Republic, inasmuch as the idea of an independent Europe with a Franco-German basis formed a clear, immediate objective on the road to the final objective, namely France's rank in world politics, particularly as compared to that of the United States. Once this immediate objective appeared to be out of reach, no other precise objective immediately presented itself. This first resulted in the replacement of a strongly articulated policy by attitudes which did not take the place of a precise action. The overture to Peking and the call for unification of Latin peoples at the time of the trip to South America in 1964 seem to have been attempts to find an alternate policy. But the French influence in Latin America was not a playable card, and the recognition of Mao Tse-tung's China did not bring the anticipated satisfactions. Therefore, there only remained the resort to a rapprochement with the USSR. The rapprochement proved to be facilitated by a series of convergent factors.

1. The Soviet Union was also considering this rapprochement as beneficial. The reaction to the recognition of China showed an almost surprising understanding, as the gesture could have been interpreted in a fashion construed to be as anti-Soviet as it was anti-American. *Izvestia* denied what "some newspapers" had called the Soviet dissatisfaction with an event which, on the contrary, perfectly satisfied the wishes of the USSR.

2. The Eastern European countries as a group, for their part, were looking for Western contacts.

3. The war in Vietnam was growing more and more important, involving the United States and also China, which enabled the USSR and France to play jointly the role of conciliatory and mediating power.

Finally, as it has been said, the Cuban Affair had deeply changed the balance of power in the world, in the eyes of General de Gaulle. For him, the Soviet Union had acknowledged the superiority of the United States, and therefore there was no longer any military danger in Europe; consequently, one could loosen the Atlantic ties and approach the USSR.

It is undoubtedly necessary to describe here in detail the Franco-Soviet contacts since 1964. In January of 1964, Valéry Giscard d'Estaing, Minister of Finance, stayed in the Soviet Union, while Constantine Rudnev, Vice-President of the Soviet Council, came to France, where he was followed in February by a Soviet parliamentary mission led by Nicolai Podgorny, Secretary of the USSR Communist Party. Then came Edgar Faure's trip to Moscow, and his stay in Peking which opened the way to recognition of Communist China. From that moment on, trips and contacts on the political,

economic, and cultural levels became increasingly frequent. After
Gromyko's visit to Paris on April 30, 1965, the most prominent
event was Couve de Murville's stay in Moscow in late October.

The trip culminated officially in three documents: an agreement
on cooperation in the study and exploration of outer space for peaceful purposes; an agreement on scientific, technical, and economic
cooperation; and a long and fairly vapid joint declaration. Of far
greater interest was the style of the trip and the content of the
President of the Republic's speeches. From Moscow to Leningrad,
from the former Stalingrad to Siberia, from battlefields of the common war to missile launching sites, General de Gaulle received a
warm welcome, which must have appeared to him as the best justification for his policy, and which incontestably flattered and excited
the French public. His speeches restated and developed the themes
previously mentioned. Thus, the address delivered at the Kremlin
on June 20:

> . . . France, for her part, is not satisfied with this rigid confronta-
> tion of the two organizations. Without ceasing, quite the con-
> trary, to be a country of freedom and a Western nation par excel-
> lence, she would like to see the harmful spell broken and, at
> least insofar as she is concerned, the start of the implementation
> of new relations with the so-called Eastern European States, to-
> ward détente, entente and cooperation.

Cooperation: General de Gaulle uses this word at every meeting
with a foreign leader. In regard to the former French colonies, its
meaning is clear: it means technical assistance and financial aid.
Relations with the countries of Black Africa are excellent. After the
sanctions imposed following the brutal expropriation of French
agricultural holdings, relations with Tunisia returned to normal in
1966. In regard to Morocco, the Ben Barka affair — the kidnapping
and doubtless the assassination in Paris of the leader of the opposition in Morocco — has darkened the atmosphere considerably. Relations with Algeria were not affected by the violent replacement in
June, 1965 of President Ben Bella by Colonel Boumedienne. The
agreement of July, 1965 on petroleum products, very advantageous

for Algeria, could even pass for a model of an oil agreement equally favorable to both parties — although Algerian oil is very expensive and serves mainly to provide France with a range of possible sources. But a Franco-Algerian crisis arose in May, 1966 because of new nationalizations ordered by the Boumedienne Government.

From 1964 on, President de Gaulle has continued his strong appeals against the division of the world into blocs, and in favor of non-engagement. This can be seen in his speech at Addis-Ababa on August 27, 1966: "Ethiopia, far from confining herself within her frontiers or absorbing herself in some political or ideological bloc, or submitting to such and such a foreign hegemony, opens herself instead deliberately to all contacts and opportunities for coopera-tion." The result is a very clear rapprochement with the United Nations, inasmuch as U Thant shares, to a great extent, General de Gaulle's views on Vietnam.

The Vietnamese war weighs heavily on Franco-American rela-tions. General de Gaulle has spoken more and more critically of United States policy, culminating in his wholly unilateral condem-nation of the US intervention, in his speech at Pnom Penh on September 1, 1966. The root of his argument lies in the parallel drawn between the withdrawal of France from Algeria, and the desire that the United States withdraw from Vietnam. By straining this comparison a bit, we can see why the Franco-American dialogue is so difficult. One French observer has written:

> It is striking to note how, by way of an odd reversal, Europe finds herself today in the same position of critic lately held by the American nation. When one has not, or when one no longer has, the responsibility for ensuring the daily existence of an over-seas country, it is easy to find, to whisper about, or to proclaim elegant and simple solutions for all problems. For fifteen years, Europe fumed against what she thought was demagogy in Amer-ican policy toward Africa and Southeast Asia, arbitrary simplifica-tions, disregard of concrete facts, and a kind of *Schadenfreude* [malicious joy] while friends labored through mud and blood. But how unerringly she has now learned to play that role.[3]

[3] Pierre Moussa, *Les États-Unis et les nations prolétaires,* Paris, Éditions du Seuil, 1965, p. 37.

Returning to the outlines of the Algerian war, and adding to it the history of the Indo-Chinese war until 1954, one is first of all struck by the similarity in official statements. First, there are the optimistic statements regularly proven wrong by the facts. This is from the statement made by Paul Coste-Floret, Minister of War, in May, 1947: "In my estimation, there is no longer any military problem in Indo-China. Our military victory is total." How many identical statements have been made by generals and ministers — and notably by McNamara! Then, the declarations announcing a hard and firm line of policy, subsequently abandoned. Talk with Ho Chi Minh? "I have always replied that the person responsible for Indo-China will never take that step," declared Mr. Letourneau in December, 1952. Negotiate with the FLN? "That I shall never do," promised General de Gaulle to the men of the barricades on January 29, 1960. The American leaders are likewise traveling down the road toward agreeing to talk with the National Liberation Front — i.e., toward the idea that in order to end a war, one must negotiate directly with one's adversary. To embark on a Suez-style expedition was to fail to recognize that the FLN was made up of Algerians; to bomb Hanoi and perhaps China tomorrow is to fail to recognize that the National Liberation Front is made up of South Vietnamese.

But is there not a radical difference between Vietnam and Algeria, in that Ho Chi Minh is a Communist while Ben Bella was not? The question merits consideration, if only to bring out the curious reversal that has taken place in Franco-American relations. Year after year, French officials and generals sought to convince the United States that Algerian nationalism also represented a communist threat, because the Vietminh had been both nationalist and communist. But today, General de Gaulle labels the Vietcong as a "form of national resistance." "Since our enemy in Algeria was basically nationalist, yours in Vietnam is also," de Gaulle now tells Washington.

The two attitudes do not reveal, however, what for twenty years has been a special characteristic of the war in Vietnam: in the whole history of decolonization, Ho Chi Minh is the only leader who, from the very beginning, was both a hero in the nationalist struggle and an experienced communist militant as well. Since 1947, and especially since the Korean War, this has given his struggle the character of a confrontation between the two blocs. And French leaders were only too happy to dwell upon that fact in order to obtain American assistance. Vincent Auriol made a special trip to Washington to explain to President Truman: "The present situation in Vietnam, where the forces of France and her allies are successfully combating communist aggression." And what a triumph for French diplomacy can be seen in the resolution adopted by NATO in December, 1952, expressing "profound admiration for the courageous combat . . . against communist aggression," and stating that "the war being fought by the forces of the French Union in Indo-China deserves the unconditional support of all Atlantic governments"!

The American leaders, who were long sympathetic to the revolutionary struggles in Africa, when they were directed against the Netherlands, Great Britain, or France in the name of anti-colonialism, appear today to have forgotten or overlooked the beginning of the story — the period to which General de Gaulle referred in his letter to Ho Chi Minh last January. The understatement is telling: "A better understanding between the French and the Vietnamese, at the close of the world war, would have prevented the cruel events which are tearing your country apart." Ben Bella was a nobody on November 1, 1954. The recognition of Algerian independence in 1962 was the fruit of a long struggle. But nine months before the Indo-Chinese war began in December, 1946, Jean Sainteny, delegate of the French High Commissioner, had signed an agreement stating: "The French Government recognizes the Republic of Vietnam as a free state. . . ."

The same Sainteny, who was severely wounded during the attack on Hanoi in December, was later to be Mendès-France's special envoy in Hanoi after the 1954 Geneva Conference, and then again the special envoy to Ho Chi Minh in August, 1966. His personal history deserves the consideration of American leaders in understanding the reaction of so many French political leaders or journalists concerned with Vietnam. For them, Ho Chi Minh cannot represent a sort of communist ringleader receiving orders from Peking, because they have had too many amiable conversations in the past with this man, so shaped by French culture, and disappointed by France twenty years ago. Nor was the example of former adjutant Ben Bella so very different in one basic respect: despite all the atrocities in Indo-China and Algeria, there remained in both wars a sort of common language between the enemies, and something more than the fact that both sides spoke French — a common language which does not in the least exist between the Americans and the Vietcong.

Ho Chi Minh is a communist. But even if the communist world were not profoundly divided today, it is not coincidental that Hanoi enjoys better relations with the Soviet Union. The real feelings of the Vietnamese toward China resemble very much the feelings of the Polish toward the USSR. Of much greater importance is the argument concerning elections and the right of self-determination of the Vietnamese people — and American leaders were justified in their consternation over de Gaulle's letter to Ho Chi Minh, demanding the right to set up a representative government only for South Vietnam. But it must be admitted that the North was not responsible for putting off ad infinitum the elections provided for in the Geneva accords. And above all, the very notion of free elections in the midst of a war is regarded in France with more skepticism than elsewhere because of the Algerian experience.

One would not strain the comparison in saying that the United States is approximately at the stage of Guy Mollet's triptyque of 1956: cease-fire, elections, negotiations (with those elected). After many hesitations, General de Gaulle had arrived in 1962 at the conclusion long advocated by others: first negotiations; then, once these have taken place, a cease-fire; and elections, which would merely ratify the agreement that had been reached. What are the real feelings of the majority of the people of South Vietnam? What were the real feelings of the majority of Algerians in 1960? No one can say with certainty. But if the minority who struggle on cannot be defeated, one must end by negotiating with them; and when one once takes that step, they will receive the support of the majority.

However sincere the US Government may be in advocating self-determination for Vietnam, its credibility was severely weakened by the intervention in San Domingo in 1965. For General de Gaulle, as for almost the entire French press, there was no relationship between the possible return to power of a legally elected president and the presence of Soviet missiles in Cuba. In expounding his "backyard theory," President Johnson spoke the cynical language of pure power and of national interest alone — while the American press and American leaders continually reproach General de Gaulle (and not without reason) for his recourse to brutal diplomatic strategies.

This is especially true in regard to financial matters. Perhaps it is since General de Gaulle carried his struggle against American domination onto financial ground that the United States has become actively hostile to his policies as a whole. His intention is indeed to weaken the privileged position of the dollar and the pound sterling. France's international financial position gives him that opportunity. In August, 1966 French reserves amounted to more than 6 billion dollars, 86 per cent of which were in gold: the 4,585 tons of gold in the hands of the Bank of France come for the most part from Fort Knox. The intentional weakening of the dollar that resulted from diminishing the gold supply backing it should not, however, make the United States forget that the Fifth Republic not only pays French debts, but pays them in advance — for instance, the repayment of 178.5 million dollars on July 1, 1965. On the whole, France's foreign debt has been reduced from 3,093 million dollars at the end of 1958 to 454.7 million in July, 1965.

It is true that, in all, France received approximately 4.5 billion dollars from the United States following the war, and that this was for the most part in the form of a gift. But American journalists and senators are wrong to counter de Gaulle's financial policies by recalling what the United States did financially for France during and following the war. It is perfectly true that everybody should be grateful to everybody. But either both wars were fought for a common cause, or they were not. If they were, the fact that one country — the major country — entered the war late, was not destroyed, and had fewer losses proportionately than her allies — all this makes it natural to share the expense. On the other hand, if it was not a common cause, if it was for American national interest alone that the US entered the war, then there should not be any question of gratitude.

General de Gaulle's policies toward the United States do not shock the majority of Frenchmen; quite the contrary! His point of departure meets with virtually no criticism — all the more because today the Soviet Union no longer appears as a threat. Precisely because France is a Western country, it is connected economically, socially, ideologically — in civilization and culture — with all Western countries. The only way for France to achieve status or independence is through a new relationship with the United States. The war in Vietnam is viewed with disapproval, in part at least out of one implicit but always present consideration. If a tremendous power like the US is unable to vanquish a small enemy without destroying the whole country, then the cause of the powerful country must not be a worthy one. And even if the cause is worthy, one meets in France with a curious reaction, which accounts for the sympathy toward Fidel Castro, and which Pierre Moussa described apropos the developing nations: "If a Rolls Royce upsets a bicyclist in a poor neighborhood, the driver must not be surprised if the crowd vehemently takes the cyclist's part, whatever the objective responsibilities might be."[4]

De Gaulle's speech in Pnom Penh brought American annoyance to its boiling point. How can one believe de Gaulle's assurances of friendship when he blames all wrongs in the Vietnam struggle on the US, when he expels US forces intended to defend his own country, when he relentlessly seeks to weaken the position of the dollar? How can one avoid considering him as an adversary? To the question: "Do you think that France is a loyal ally of the United States?", 32 per cent of the Americans interviewed replied "Yes," and 35 per cent "No" in 1963. Three years later, the respective figures were 16 per cent and 56 per cent.[5] But in the meantime, the French are less and less interested in being the "loyal ally." Last April, 35 per

---

[4] Moussa, *op cit.,* p. 60.

[5] Gallup poll, released by the Institut français d'opinion publique (IFOP); quoted in *Paris Presse,* July 20, 1966.

cent of those interviewed in France by the IFOP considered that the fundamental interests of France and the United States were similar, while 43 per cent considered them different. Nineteen per cent thought that, given the present state of the world, France should be on the side of the United States; 9 per cent on the side of the Soviet Union; 57 per cent replied "Neither side."[6] And it is also true that to the question: "How much confidence do you have in the United States ability to lead the West wisely?" only 2 per cent replied "very solid confidence"; 20 per cent more or less confidence; 35 per cent not very much confidence; and 22 per cent very little confidence.

The desire to maintain a certain distance in relations with the United States began as a theme of the Left in 1948, was taken up by the Right in 1958, and has again returned as an important aspect in the "Leftist" position. This can be seen in a declaration signed in May, 1966 by twenty public figures, who are extremely critical of de Gaulle's domestic policies and the *force de frappe:*

> As dedicated partisans of the political and economic construction of Europe, we cannot remain satisfied with the ambiguous formulas which spell out the dependence of Europe on the American economy and American policies. In accord with a great number of voters of the Left, and in accord with the majority of the forces for progress in the world, we support an international policy of peace founded on the refusal to be integrated into hegemonial blocs, on an enlarged and reunited Europe, and on cooperation with the countries of the "third world" and the nonaligned nations — the policy which is currently being pursued in the name of France.

Among those subscribing to the declaration were André Philip, a devoted partisan of European integration for more than twenty years; Pierre Le Brun, until this year non-communist head of the *Confédération Générale du Travail,* the major French trade union (communist dominated); and the writer David Rousset, who was the first person to denounce the Soviet concentration camps. In July,

[6] Poll conducted by the Institut français d'opinion publique, published in *France-Soir,* May 8, 1966.

the Federation of the Democratic and Socialist Left (*Fédération de la Gauche Démocratique et Socialiste*), headed by François Mitterand, de Gaulle's major opponent in the presidential elections, made public its program. In regard to foreign policy, they declared their opposition to the *force de frappe;* but concerning NATO:

> The changes which have taken place since 1949 in the situation of the members of the Atlantic Alliance necessitate indeed — even in the interest of the Alliance's cohesiveness — a thorough reorganization. A government of the Left would engage in negotiations with its fourteen partners, in order to reappraise each member's responsibilities in the situations the Alliance might face in the coming years. Since France has left NATO, we must explore henceforth the possibilities for organizing a workable peaceful coexistence, in order to determine precisely the extent and value of the military agreements which the NATO allies will conclude among themselves.

In June, an excellent political cartoon[7] portrayed de Gaulle and Mitterand as two boxers sitting in a ring, each with his trainer at his side. Mitterand's trainer was Waldeck-Rochet, secretary-general of the French communist party; de Gaulle's was Kosygin: one could not better illustrate how de Gaulle's foreign policy poses problems for the Left. The same holds true for the opposition on the Right: the rapprochement with the communist bloc and the withdrawal from NATO operations might be viewed with consternation or irritation; but how could a group which has traditionally cherished national glory possibly remain impassive before the French people's reaction to de Gaulle's policies? On the eve of the presidential elections in November, 1965, the French Institute of Public Opinion inquired: "Do you feel that in the past seven years, General de Gaulle has had a good influence, a bad influence, or no influence at all in regard to the standard of living in France? And the status of France in the world? And the way France is governed? And social questions?" The reply "a good influence" was given by 37 per cent on social questions, by 48 per cent on the standard of living,

---

[7] Cf. *L'Express,* June 20, 1966.

by 57 per cent on the governing of France — and by 76 per cent on France's world position. (Seven per cent replied "a bad influence," and 4 per cent "none at all.")[8]

One can, of course, raise the question posed by Maurice Faure in the National Assembly in November, 1964:

> You are always referring to the prestige of General de Gaulle: he is great, very great, and probably one would have to go back very far to find an example of a French head of state of such great prestige. But what influence do you have in Washington, in London, in Bonn, in Rome and in the Benelux capitals . . . ? What role of arbitration do you play in the Congo, in Cyprus, in South Vietnam?[9]

In fact, prestige and influence are not necessarily correlaries. Without prestige, it is true, influence is limited. Prestige, however, does not suffice to create influence. In principle, it paves the way for action, and does not replace action. It seems, however, that today the Fifth Republic has entered a phase in which the quest for prestige has turned into an end in itself.

But one must include two additional comments on prestige. The first concerns the curious inability of American public opinion — including public leaders — to apply to collective psychology what is constantly reiterated regarding the individual: man does not live by bread alone, but likewise by respect and consideration. One's social status does not depend on one's standard of living alone, but also on the respect and consideration of other people. Is this not also true of peoples?

In Latin America, Africa, or France, the notion of independence represents far more than a purely political concept: striving for prosperity is not everything — the desire to affirm one's own existence in the presence of a more powerful entity also plays an important role. When the Soviet Union accepts the French system of color television, when the US does not accept the Caravelle and the Concorde, it is not merely economic realities that are involved:

[8] Cf. the review *Sondages*, 1966, I, p. 21.
[9] *Journal officiel, Assemblée Nationale*, 1964, p. 4428.

there is also the satisfaction of one's self-esteem at stake in the one case, and the resentment of a power which uses its might abusively in the other.

The second consideration is that prestige can of itself create influence. To be sure, distrust of General de Gaulle has reached new heights today in Washington, Bonn, Brussels, The Hague, and London — even when de Gaulle is right, there is little chance of his being listened to in these capitals. But at the same time, to some extent in all parts of the world, his positions and attitudes are gathering a growing number of admirers. Prestige or influence?

In my personal capacity as a French citizen participating in French political life, I might appraise the foreign policy of the Fifth Republic severely. But an objective appraisal of its record must take into account a considerable number of achievements; must take note of the fact that it is to some extent irreversible; and — in a presentation intended for the American public — must emphasize how much US policies and attitudes over the past twenty-five years have actually contributed to what Americans, from Washington to San Francisco, consider most shocking about Gaullism.

Alfred Grosser is Director of Studies and
Research at the National Foundation of Political Science in Paris and a Professor at the
Institute of Political Studies, University of
Paris. He also teaches at the Bologna Center
of Johns Hopkins University's School of
Advanced International Studies. He is a
regular contributor to Le Monde, and writes
on foreign policy for the Catholic daily, La
Croix. In 1965 he taught at Stanford University.